CLOSE THE DEAL AND SUDDENLY GROW RICH

What Others Said ...

"A friend from the media asked me the other day, off the record, how good Marco Robinson really is [in closing deals and helping others to do likewise]. I told him without hesitation, 'He's really that good. I'd put him right up there with Ziglar, Mandino, Tracy, Girard and Bettger.' I believe his books will become classics and mandatory reading for anyone who wants to excel in sales and closing deals—period."

—**Immanuel Lim**, business owner and publisher

"Whether you're a seasoned salesperson or you're taking your first tentative steps into the dynamic world of selling, when you read this book, know that you're in safe hands. There is something for everyone and when you follow the process Marco Robinson outlines, your results will skyrocket. Marco is a consummate professional, a person of extraordinary ability and someone who is totally passionate about other people's success. Read it and you'll be well rewarded."

—**Paul Counsel, Ph.D.**, Author, Wealth Specialist & Artist
(www.paulcounsel.com.au)

"*Know When To Close The Deal And Suddenly Grow Rich*! is not just a book but you're getting Marco Robinson's valuable years of experience, techniques and most importantly, his mindset of success! If you're looking for ways to achieve breakthroughs in selling, this is the man who understands salesmanship and communication more than anyone else I've ever met, period. Most books will just teach you the techniques of selling and leave you 'empty' at the end of reading—but not in this book. Not only will you uncover new strategies behind the concept of selling, you'll also discover your hidden potential that will lead you to greater business and personal wealth."

—**Patric Chan**, International Speaker, World-Renowned Internet Marketer
& Author of the bestseller, 72 Amazing Ways To Internet Marketing
(www.PatricChan.com)

"I've known Marco Robinson since 2002 when I met him at a seminar. I picked him as my buddy out of over 1,000 people. Why? To this day I'm not sure. I do know that my life has never been quite the same since. I've never met anyone who comes close to Marco when it comes to energy, personality and persuasive power. In terms of his ability to influence, Marco is simply irresistible! I'm very proud to have been asked to recommend this book which I believe is destined to take its place amongst the sales classics. I couldn't put it down! The only complaint I have is that HE DIDN'T WRITE IT SOONER! I think this does the job and I mean every word."

—**Dr Bob Scott, Ph.D.**, Emergency Physician

"From the initial re-launch of the Tanco vacation club products in late 1997, from a week-based ownership to the Vacation SuperClub points-based product, Marco Robinson was hand-picked to lead as the day-to-day Project Director heading a further hand-picked expat team covering all of the major departmental areas of Sales Management, Marketing, Collections, Customer Care and Reservations.

"Commencing with onsite sales at Duta Vista with offsite locations in Bangsar, Port Dickson, Rawang, Kuantan and Brunei, the 1998 target was for RM32 million in sales. Under the leadership of the Tanco board and Consulting Director, Marco steered his team into surpassing this to reach a record-breaking RM72 mil in sales for the year.

"With resorts located in Kuala Lumpur, Kuantan, Port Dickson, Rawang, Australia and New Zealand, the club grew beyond everyone's expectations with Marco striving for greater goals daily. At the 1999 ARDA convention in Florida, the Tanco name was starting to be heard.

"In 1999, with an annual target set for $100 mil in sales and a further product introduced at Vacation WorldClub, the group grew to over 12 resort locations (owned and controlled) and strategic alliance resorts also started to be developed. This also grew to encompass new sales decks with Malaysia to cope with the unprecedented growth.

"By ARDA 2000, in Las Vegas, Tanco was asked to speak on the unprecedented success that had been achieved in Asia.

"With Marco's team smashing annual budgets Tanco became the largest vacation ownership club in Asia and boasted in excess of 32,000 members in just 4 short years."

—**Stuart Ockenden**, Vice President, Operations and Business Development of Tanco Resorts Bhd (1998 - 2001)

"I want to express my utmost GRATITUDE to you. I've benefited a lot from reading your book. With zero sales background, I've closed a deal on my first corporate appointment ON THE SPOT. The prospect was so excited and happy with my offer, they went to the ATM machine IMMEDIATELY and gave me $8,100 CASH!"

—**Lai May Leng**

"Best book I have ever read. Transformed my results, and would you believe it, I now managed to put a deposit down on a new condo because of Marco! Truly inspirational, very effective, practical and AWESOME. Don't miss the workshop with the book, it will SAVE your life!"

—**Sherifah Alsagoff**

"I had an amazing breakthrough at the book workshop when Marco interrupted my pattern. Sometimes we need a person to give it to your face for that paradigm shift. If you need that desire to boost your sales, read the book and go to the workshop. I closed two deals on the day after attending the workshop and got referrals without even asking for them!!!"

—**Kay Morris**

"Last year when I started to learn from Marco Robinson I was a housewife with little income. In my first month I made $49,000 without breaking sweat and now I am enjoying income residually every month. I am also the proud owner of a brand-new BMW coupe because of what I learned from Marco!!!"
Rita Baratharaj

"Wish I had this program 20 years ago (but not too late)! Marco showed the way to a wonderful and satisfied life. It was life changing."

—**KS Wong**

"I've increased my knowledge towards financial independence. Marco was superb."

—**Shayamala Davi**

"Loved his energy, humor and I learned the first steps towards a different approach to attitude in life."

—**Soo San**

"Very informative speaker, extremely good—the best I would say—and I learnt a lot from Mr. Marco ... eye opening and life changing ... will definitely come back for more!"

—**Siti Asmilih Ahmad**

"If we conquer our fear and limitations we can achieve wealth ... if we have a good mentor. Marco is a motivating speaker ... Speaker is awesome and the program is good. I rate the content life changing!"

—**Tiger Cheong**

"Great! I will recommend him to friends and business partners."

—**Warren Wong**

"It's a mind-blowing experience and Marco seems to have a lot of knowledge."

—**Mohammed Nasih**

"Marco shared real-life experience which is inspiring. The zero-down payment for property is useful."

—**Tan Sai Hup**

"Extraordinary! Have learnt a lot!"

—**Polly Koh**

"He (Marco) is a dynamic entrepreneur with a global vision and has clarity. In short he is a trendsetter and an astute businessman."

—**Dr Mahesan Subrememan**

"It (the seminar) gave me the idea how to generate income through property investment ... the speaker is very motivational and inspiring."

—**Ratnabuman, R**

"Marco excellent. Program excellent."

—**Michael Foong**

"Shattered age-old business misconceptions. Business edge tools revealed. Awesome!"

—**Victor Liew**

"Marco is very confident and very daring. I thought it was life changing."

—**Pam Tan**

"Amazing and full of new knowledge. Would recommend to friends."

—**Linda Jalil**

"Tremendously amazing. It (the program) really wakes me up—an amazing guy!"
Norazlyzan Ramli
"Very good. Would recommend to friends because of the benefits [Marco shares]. Excellent."

—**Samsurijan Mat Salleh**

"I would recommend for my friends to change their mindset. Marco's transparency and willingness to share his hands-on experience was superb!"

—**Mohamed Yusoff**

"Powerful!"

—**Chin Chee Kong**

"I would recommend to all my friends. It (the seminar) changed the way I think. 5 out 5!"

—**Chin Pei Jun**

"Marco was refreshing, energetic and straightforward. I will recommend my friends because it will change their mindset."

—**Mohd Sunny Abdullah**

"The most valuable thing I learned at Marco's workshop was the opportunities on how to make my first million."

—**D B Kamaruddin**

"Valuable. Very good."

—**Mohd D Ismail**

"I'm going to recommend Marco to my friends so that they can live the life they want. I love Marco's way of presenting!"

—**Syaham**

"…ideas I have never known before. Excellent seminar workshop!"

—**Kenny Damian**

"I loved Marco's excitement and energy and his 'can do' attitude. Excellent!"

—**V Navaratnam**

"Goals and objectives was the most valuable thing I learned. Spot on. Mind blowing!"

—**Kelvin Oi**

"Marco is excellent. Super energetic and I thought the content was excellent."

—**Ahmed Suhaimi**

"…encouraging experience…recommend to my friends to help them too…most motivational."

—**Syed Mahmood**

"Today's experience was awesome. Marco is a great guy with self-championship. I'm very lucky today to see and get the experience of the most successful man."

—**Sivaraj**

CLOSE THE DEAL
AND
SUDDENLY
GROW RICH

The Ground Breaking
#1 Bestseller That Can
Skyrocket Your Sales
Results in 24 Hours

MARCO ROBINSON

NEW YORK

LONDON • NASHVILLE • MELBOURNE • VANCOUVER

CLOSE THE DEAL AND SUDDENLY GROW RICH
The Ground Breaking #1 Bestseller That Can Skyrocket Your Sales Results in 24 Hours

© 2018 MARCO ROBINSON

Published in New York, New York, by Morgan James Publishing. Morgan James is a trademark of Morgan James, LLC. www.MorganJamesPublishing.com

The right of Marco Robinson to be identified as author of this work has been asserted by him in accordance with section 77 and 78 of the Copyright, Designs and Patents Act 1988.

The Morgan James Speakers Group can bring authors to your live event. For more information or to book an event visit The Morgan James Speakers Group at www.TheMorganJamesSpeakersGroup.com.

ISBN 978-1-68350-911-0 paperback
ISBN 978-1-68350-912-7 eBook
Library of Congress Control Number: 2017919144

Cover Design by:
Rachel Lopez
www.r2cdesign.com

Interior Design by:
Bonnie Bushman
The Whole Caboodle Graphic Design

In an effort to support local communities, raise awareness and funds, Morgan James Publishing donates a percentage of all book sales for the life of each book to Habitat for Humanity Peninsula and Greater Williamsburg.

Get involved today! Visit
www.MorganJamesBuilds.com

TABLE OF CONTENTS

PREFACE

On October 31, 1989, I went to the ATM machine praying there was money I could withdraw. Two pounds 71 pence was all I had. I will never forget that day. After four weeks of "trying" to sell, I ended up with no hope, no prospects, exhausted, no friends, no car, and no money... until my life changed in 24 hours.

In seven days I became top salesperson in the company, salesperson of the year, then Sales and Marketing Director of the group and got headhunted every day!

Basically, I went from a very shy, miserable, spotty ginger-haired guy to a successful spotty ginger-haired guy with lots of money. Beautiful women wanted to "hang out" with me, I had a beautiful, expensive sports car and the best clothes money could buy at the age of 22!

What if you could propel your sales results into orbit and be financially free within the next 12 months just by reading a few chapters of this book and internalizing the principles? I was given a similar book when I was 21 years old. I read it, read it again, and kept on reading it. And in 24 hours, from being the saddest loser you could ever meet, with no hope whatsoever, I became a Champion Closer, top of the tree! If I can do it, you can do it too!

In this book, you will have the tools and psychology to beat the odds again and again!

My advice?

Read it, trust yourself, and use it every day, and I guarantee, you will be very glad you made the choice to ask for help! I am here to help you never to have to worry about poor sales and money problems ever again!

INTRODUCTION

"A Brief History of Perfectly Timed Closes"

Before we begin, let me give you a quick preview on how this book can help you double your sales within the next four weeks by learning what to ask, when to ask it, and when to listen. First off, let me share with you three events that really happened and exactly what was said.

"The Smoking Close": Case I

Me:	Would you prefer luxury holidays for the rest of your life or lung cancer?
	The Prospect sits in silence for around 20 seconds absorbing the shock of the question then looks at his wife, then they both turn to me.
Prospect:	HOLIDAYS!
Me:	Then put your cigarette out (passing him the ashtray) and put your John Hancock here and you too ma'am.

They sign paperwork.

Deal Value:	$17,500
Time spent with clients:	1 minute
Date:	July 17, 1991
Place:	Manchester, England
My Age at the time:	23
My position:	Sales Manager
Company:	Global Marketing Europe (UK) Ltd
Product:	Timeshare

How did I know when to close this deal? Would you like to learn the tools that I used which created millions of dollars of income for me?

If you want to be a champion closer instead of an average producer this book is for you.

"The Prevention Close": Case II

Me:	Would you like your patients to know about their disease too early or late?
Prospect:	(A doctor) Without a doubt too early.
Me:	I think I'd like to be your patient. Which training course date do you prefer, July or October?
Prospect:	October.
Me:	How would you like to pay, credit card or cash?
Prospect:	Cash, but I don't have it with me.
Me:	How would you like to get it to us, bank transfer or pay cash now?
Prospect:	Cash now, it's at home. Can you wait here for me while I go and get it?
Me:	Absolutely, just before you go and do that please help me complete your application form, it'll just take 30 seconds.
Prospect:	Okay, no problem.
Me:	Thanks very much. Just put the 10 per cent deposit on your card, and we will do the rest later.
Prospect:	Of course. (Processes card) Be back in an hour.
Me:	Look forward to it. See you shortly.

Deal Value:	$100,000
Time spent with client:	9 minutes
Date:	August 10, 2007
Place:	Kuala Lumpur, Malaysia
Product:	Bloodscan wellness benchmarking tool
My position:	Bloodscan Malaysia Master license holder

And, yes, before you ask. The doctor did come back and brought $ 90,000 in a plastic bag and gave it to me. I will tell you the rest of this story later and the sheer hilarity my colleagues experienced when this lovely doctor came back with a plastic bag full of cash! They simply didn't believe it would happen, and when it did, their jaws dropped into the basement car park!

"The No-Risk Close": Case III

Me:	My question to you is this. If you could improve your sales results by 50 per cent within the first seven days after attending this workshop, would you invest the necessary funds?
Prospect:	Excuse me?
Me:	You heard exactly what I said. If I could guarantee you that your sales results will double within the first seven days of attending this workshop, would you join today?
Prospect:	(Pauses for some time.) Would you put that in writing?
Me:	Absolutely. I'll do even better than that, I'll write a personal note to you and sign that guarantee.
Prospect:	Here, put all of it on my credit card. (Passes my assistant the card, deal is processed.)

Deal Value:	$3,500
Time spent with prospect:	3 minutes
Date:	March 10, 2004
Place:	Cititel Hotel, Mid Valley Mega Mall, Malaysia
Product:	My seminar package "Total Wealth"
My position:	Creator and owner.

Okay, let's start with the above close. And before you think I made it up, you're wrong. This really did happen.

I could have used a hundred other closes on this gentleman, but I didn't because my champion closer instincts told me different.

Think of being a champion closer like being a fine musician. A fine musician knows the right tune and knows how to hit the right notes only after practicing for many hours.

The amazing thing was that this guy had attended six other sales seminar previews and never been asked this question before. It's not a rocket science question; it's a question and close that's easy to learn, so easy anyone can do it. It was because I asked it at the right time and with the correct tone, confidence, and body language, and also had no fear of a negative outcome (and that's important), that it was delivered naturally and with no effort at all.

His whole buying psychology was focused on whether he would be making a huge mistake spending his hard-earned money on something that may not work for him.

People's biggest fear in buying anything is that they are going to make a mistake and look foolish.

Once I removed that fear, he had no hesitation in committing and spending his money. And I meant what I said about the guarantee. I would always stand by this, and he knew it. That's why he was so relieved to hand his money over!

Now of course in the guarantee I gave him, I did stipulate that he must practice and role-play the skills he would be learning to a level of total internalization, meaning he knew it backwards and forwards and I had to test him first. That made sense to him. Some guarantees don't do this, leaving the students expecting miracles and a genie to come out of a lamp and magically gift them all the tools. It never happens. This is not magic; it's a process that can be learned, and learned very quickly!

In the case mentioned above, it would have been riskier if I hadn't said that when I did. The prospect would have walked away and his life would have been worse because of it. I had total faith in what I was doing and believed if he didn't join us I would be doing him an injustice, an injustice that would have set him back years. I didn't want him to go through that pain.

You see, sometimes you spend hours with a prospect. You visit them ten times, give them tons of facts and figures, build rapport with them, get to know them, blah, blah, blah. And it can still result in a no-sale. How much time have you wasted here, and how many other prospects could you have closed while working on this?

The fact is that Darren—yes, I still remember his name—had listened and attended at least six other seminar previews in the space of two weeks and still had not purchased a ticket. He just couldn't decide. At the preview for my seminar, I saw my staff spend the longest time with this guy. He was the last one remaining from over a hundred other people, many of whom had already purchased a ticket.

It was now an hour after the presentation had finished, and to be honest, he was just asking the same questions over again and again. All the objections had been handled. Then one of my staff approached me and said, "Marco, I know you normally don't do this, but this man is really interested. Could you talk to him? I don't think he can afford it, but he really wants it."

So I walked over and was introduced to him. My staff told me all about him, his background, how many previews he had attended and so on. The rest is history, as they say.

Was he shocked? Oh yes, absolutely. But the great thing is he actually thanked me for having the gumption to say what I said. And his life got better and better because he made the commitment to attend one of my programs. In fact, he was so happy he attended all of my programs and even started selling for me, because he said he wanted to help others! This was all because I closed him **at the right time, with the right words for him. Words he needed to hear to make the decision for him!**

How do you know what to say and when to say it? That's the question I get asked all the time. What I can tell you is I learned it. And I learned it so well that it became an instinct, a kind of radar that has never failed me. Yes, I know when you read about the closes I mentioned above, they look really easy, don't they? You know what? It is easy when it becomes a habit, and no, it wasn't easy at first!

Without a certain amount of struggle there can be no success.

How long did it take me to become as good as I am now? Well, it took me three months of struggle then it just got better and better. Could you live with that?

Actually, when you start reading this book and practice the principles on a daily basis, it will take you a week to improve your sales. This book can assist you in closing your next prospect, and if that prospect is scheduled in tomorrow, then it can work faster than a week.

You don't need to shout, force, cajole, use amazing tricks, or work hours and hours. You just need to learn when to ask the right questions, when to listen, when to present your ideas, and to know when they really like what you have offered them.

You don't need much energy, any sweat or tears. All you need to do is **be prepared to learn the right way in doing something to achieve a certain result**. If you want to triple your sales results or multiply them by a thousand then you have to do things in a certain way that will get the results you want. That's called learning to be **effective**.

If you just keep "trying harder" with what you already know and expect different results, then you are living in a room with no windows. This will lead you nowhere.

I have been in sales for almost 20 years, pushing to make it my life's mission to discover the best results I can achieve. My determination to study has made me literally millions of dollars—not billions, just millions. As a matter of fact, the total sales I have achieved to date is close to the $500 million dollar mark.

To improve your sales results you must learn from someone who has already achieved the results you desire.

Many people are not willing to learn from a mentor and wonder why they can't achieve that certain goal in front of them. Yes, there are people have taken my courses and my advice and yet there was no improvement. Do you know why? It was because they were not willing to follow the road-map which I had given them. They refused to change how they did things! They believed in only one way—their way. Now if their way got better results than what I could get, I would want to learn from them, no doubt about it. If there was a better way, I would definitely use it to achieve better results! However, I have not yet found a better way!

What you read here in this book is nearly 20 years of experience, experience that has seen me make a lot of mistakes, too many to mention. But it was from those mistakes that I learned how to improve my sales techniques. I also learned from my mentors who were achievers, studying their methods and applying them with my own personality.

I got a better pay-check each time I learned a new skill. And when it boils down to it, friends, it doesn't matter what this book costs. What matters most is the return on your money, the wealth you will attain on your investment obtained by the skills I will teach you.

If you can make more money with minimal effort, isn't the content worth reading?

Heck, if there was a guarantee to improve my wealth by reading, I would not hesitate. Every single page, word, and advice would be worth the time. I would use it as a success bible and carry it with me always, because I know doing so will make me more money.

When I increase my wealth, I will have more freedom with my time. That, my friends, is the pure essence of financial freedom.

The simple truth is this: people make money by buying and selling items at a profit. That is how you create wealth. Carlos Slim, one of the richest men in the world, does that with a telecommunication company in Mexico. He buys and sells airtime. Bill Gates, the other richest man in the world, does that with software. Warren Buffet does it with stocks and Donald Trump does it with property.

Yes they are smart, but they are also great communicators. And I can tell you, that is the first rule in improving your sales results.

Ninety percent of your success will come down to how well you communicate and how well you use the words in your vocabulary.

That will determine how well you can sell an idea and at the same time make complete sense to your customers.

You can only close people when they are ready (i.e. they really desire what you've got) to be asked to buy what you are offering. And, yes, you will still have to ask them!

Now I know what you're thinking. You've read this other book recently that says you don't have to close or ask your prospects to buy, they'll just buy what you have. I've also read those books and some of them are very good indeed. However, you still need to guide your customer on when to buy and what to buy, and then ask for their credit card, because if you don't ask, they're not going give it to you!

However, when you do finally ask them to buy your product, it won't even feel like you closed a deal at all. It will feel naturally right because you are providing something the customer needs now to improve their life in some way or another. And if you are selling the correct product or service, they will thank you for it more than you can possibly fathom! And, more importantly, they will refer their most trusted friends to you!

Of course if you are selling a product that they don't need, they simply will not buy it, no matter how you try. Even if by some amazing pitch you do manage to get them to buy, they will cancel the order as soon as you are out of sight.

If they can't see your product benefiting them, they will not see themselves using it. Then they will definitely not buy it!

If you have been in sales, you have experienced cancellations. It doesn't feel good, does it? But it is also a gift! How come? Because your customer is telling you by their actions that you have not been professional in your presentation and that you have left some of their questions unanswered.

Average salespeople don't perceive this as a failure. They see it as a defeat. Their average sales manager will say to them, "Try harder next time," in which case, they will just show more enthusiasm but still end up making the same mistakes! This in return will get them more cancellations! Then they leave and decide that sales is not for them because they are not making any money!

You may laugh, but I can tell you from experience, this happens all the time!

If as a sales professional you are willing to take a different attitude when you get a cancellation, if you are willing to study this book and review the presentation you just did with objective eyes—that means taking the emotion out of the equation—you might uncover an error or a pattern that's simply not working for you!

This book will help you find these ineffective patterns and give you new ones that will transform your results.

Sometimes, just by reading one chapter, the difference made to your sales results will be staggering. I know it sounds audacious and a bit over the top, but just indulge yourself and have the courage to read it. I promise when you do, you will read the next chapter with gusto because you know it will make the difference between huge success and dismal failure!

I repeat, to get the results that you want, you will have to do things in a certain way. That certain way will definitely be different from the way which you have been doing it.

It's all simple common sense when it comes down to it. It really isn't that difficult. It is easy making money through sales. Spending 16 years in school may not have helped you achieve your desired results, and that is why you chose to buy this book.

Learn to get better results from the people who already have them (and these people may not be your parents or your drinking buddies!).

I do apologize for changing the subject here, but do you want the truth or a bunch of baloney that reads well? All of us got off to a bad start, friends. School did not prepare us to sell or persuade even though we do have to do that every day of our lives!

Sooner or later, you will have to persuade someone into thinking the way you think or you'll get downtrodden for the rest of your life and wonder what happened.

Successful people make things happen! Now it's your turn to learn how to make your sales happen.

BEFORE WE START...
MASTER YOUR B.R.A.N.D.

In this book, you will have the opportunity to learn information which can be used practically in your everyday life and literally transform your results and skyrocket your sales!

Before you start this journey, it is my pleasure and duty to share with you why and how you must always put your **personal brand** in front of everything else. Your brand is more than your name—it conveys who you are, your character, your attitude, your capabilities, and most importantly, if you are a potential **resource** and **benefit** to your prospects.

We are here to **serve**. Prospects are not looking for another salesperson; they are looking for someone who can **make a significant difference that can be measured**. They are looking for a resource they can trust, someone who is congruent in what he or she says and will back it up with action that is relevant to any promise he or she has made. However, this type of salesperson is amazingly rare. Why? Because if you have ever had any training as a salesperson, you were trained to hit targets and get the job done by seeing as many prospects as possible and closing them—and then move on.

We now live in a world where there has never been so much transparency. Social networks, such as Facebook, Instagram, twitter, with billions of users, are making it very easy to discover the truth behind how good your product or service really is and essentially how good you really are!

I have discovered after many years that the results in our life, including the dollars and cents, truly come from our own **b.r.a.n.d.** and I have made a simple five-step learning tool, that anyone can master. In fact, the power of this brand-new, five-step process can anchor you to your success better than any other tool out there. I urge you to internalize and use it because it will lead you to outrageous success!

Your B.R.A.N.D.

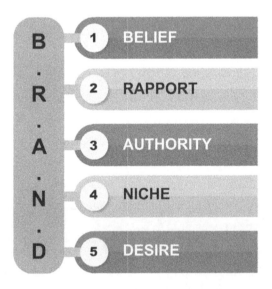

B	1 BELIEF
R	2 RAPPORT
A	3 AUTHORITY
N	4 NICHE
D	5 DESIRE

Simplicity makes your sales easy to improve, because with each of the five steps above you know what you must do to close the deal.

Generally, if you don't achieve or work on the five steps above, something very major will be missing from your sales process. That is why I have not given you a 20-step process. This five-step process will come automatically and logically when you focus on your **B.R.A.N.D.** in all of your actions, moves that will lead to tremendous success, accolades, and becoming a true Champion Closer.

Later in Chapter 3 I will briefly talk about Aristotle's famous four-step process: **A.I.D.A. (Attention-Interest-Desire-Action)**.

To complete Aristotle's most effective teaching, I would recommend you follow **B.R.A.N.D.** before you can complete **A.I.D.A.** Please allow me to clarify what I mean.

Getting great attention means saying one line that can really grab your prospects, such as if you were selling vacation incentives, which is what one of my companies does, you could say, "I supply $2,000 vacations from only $50!"

When you say this congruently and with total belief, you will attract great attention. But if you say it weakly and not confidently, it will work the opposite way, so firstly:

1. BELIEF attracts attention!

We will discuss **personal power** later, translating as you must know yourself, believe in yourself, and believe in the company you are representing and of course the products or services you are selling. The message you broadcast must be congruent—you mean what you say and your prospects know you mean it!

A lack of belief is the fundamental reason most salespeople give up and think sales is not for them! Believe it or not, I used to believe that selling was not for me! How wrong I was! I just had no belief in myself until I was desperate to be successful, then suddenly, literally overnight, I found more belief than I had ever had, and it transformed me into a super salesperson, who loves sales! You will read how I found that belief later in this book.

When you have that spine-tingling, goose-bump belief in yourself, people will pay you attention, your broadcast is unmissable—they will not want to change the channel!

2. RAPPORT inspires trust!

To further raise interest and earn the right to share some of the benefits of what you are offering, achieving a good level of **rapport** is a necessity. Rapport will strongly reduce ADD (attention deficient disorder) and help you get them to listen to you and therefore build incredible levels of **trust**.

Ask open questions and listen intently… until you literally inspire them to ask you questions. We will discuss this in great detail in this book and you must keep reading those chapters, like you must keep breathing oxygen.

When they start to like you they will automatically be interested in knowing more about you and what you do.

They will only like you when they know you understand them. This is the secret of building strong rapport! I repeat, RAPPORT is achieved only when your prospects know and believe you understand them!

3. AUTHORITY removes fear and establishes you as their resource!

The beautiful thing about knowing **B.R.A.N.D.** is that it is so easy to remember, as each step will flow into the next.

Naturally, when you have raised their interest level, they will want to know logically if you are genuine and are an expert in your field, whether your expertise can assist them in solving their problems and facilitate an easier lifestyle for them whether at home, at play, at work, or in business. This translates into the real difference you can make and they will be able to measure that difference **tangibly** (with a metric, a percentage increase especially if you are selling B2B in corporate sales) and **intangibly** (how it feels to them emotionally across all their sensory measurements: sight, taste, hearing, touch, and smell).

When you have established yourself as the "doctor" of what you do, you will establish yourself as an **authority**. And people trust experts first. Even if they have a second opinion they will always come back to you, because you have created an indispensable need for your counsel in their decision-making processes in your industry. They know you will make a positive measured difference in their lives!

This also inspires your best customers to give you great **referrals** because they know the people they are referring will benefit from your expertise. This makes them feel good and even increases their own self-esteem because they are genuinely helping out their friends. This is one of the coolest benefits from mastering your **B.R.A.N.D.** The number of salespeople who have shared with me that their customers are now giving them referrals without them asking for it is staggering! It is something you will love to experience!

4. NICHE determines value and relevance!

You may be an expert at what you do, but is your niche relevant to your prospects' needs? Does your product or service do it for them completely? Will it increase their efficiency, their results, or change their lifestyle for the better?

In the world of corporate selling, getting in the door is more challenging because your target prospects have about 60 hours of work on their desk, overwhelming deadlines to meet, and don't have time to make appointments with salespeople!

What they want to know fast is if your service or product is relevant to them in their industry, whether it can help achieve tangible metrics to increase their bottom line quickly. This, of course, is more relevant the more desperate the client is or the more pressing their need is. For example, if a division of a company needs to hit its sales target for the year by December 31 and it is now October 31 and they are 40 percent from their target, they will be more desperate to find a **resource** that can help them achieve it. This is referred to as a "triggered event," meaning a time when the resource is more critically needed.

Where does your niche come in? Well, if you can demonstrate when you want to get an appointment with your prospect, that you helped a direct competitor of theirs achieve a similar result in the same time-frame, you would become highly relevant to them. Your **niche** would attract them so powerfully, they would only "see" your offering and niche and would not waste their time with anybody else!

In corporate selling, research is more relevant, because you need to find out what that company needs. And when you can present a possible solution to them over a quick phone call, you can literally enjoy amazing results.

The highest **value** and **relevance** to your prospects is if their direct competitor has used your product or service and has enjoyed a metric increase in sales. It is relevant because they will think, if their competitor can increase their sales by 21 percent so can they! And you could be their "ticket" to huge success.

So, to get an appointment quickly with a corporate prospect, you could say something like, "Mr. Smith, one of our clients, XX Engineering, has just increased their sales by 24.6 percent using our latest CRM software program. We think we can help you achieve similar results, if not better. I think it would be prudent for us to meet and discuss—is this Friday okay?"

Any product or service can be communicated in this way. This approach is the most relevant to the targeted corporate prospects. And don't worry if you don't have on your books one of their competitors as a client. You can always relate industry case studies to them through effective research. Your niche and the delivery of your niche results will set you apart from the crowd significantly.

If you are selling products to individuals, the same relevance rule applies. The higher the relevance, the higher the perceived value of what you are offering.

You can increase the relevance and value of what you sell by presenting super success stories of other people who have positively benefited from using your product or service. The highest relevance will be achieved when that super success story is of someone they know personally—the closer the more powerful. It triggers the mindset of: "Well if my friend has used it and she is also a housewife about the same age as me, and she is also divorced and got those benefits, why can't I?"

They will demand to buy from you!

Even if you have not sold to anyone your prospects know personally, you can still generate high relevance by sharing with them testimonials of other people they can relate to who have also benefited.

It is astounding how so many so-called salespeople do not value the relevance of doing this. (Pun intended!) Yet it could literally change their results overnight—it certainly did mine!

5. DESIRE creates demands!

Belief, Rapport, Authority, and the relevance of your Niche will lead you and your prospects into focusing all your efforts on creating a sufficient motivating desire for them to buy into your offering with confidence.

You do this by sharing benefits in an expert fashion that is relevant to them and in a manner that appeals to them, i.e. in a way they can "see" themselves benefiting because you have already "seen" your prospects benefiting in your own mind like a video recording or a movie. How well you translate this movie to them will determine how much desire your prospects will have for your offering. This is because you know their DBM (dominant buying motive—the compelling reason to buy from you now!) and you really understand what they want and why they want it, and you have taken the time to build that understanding by using **B.R.A.N.D.** as your resource!

I will take you through this entire process, step by step, later in this book. The science is easy once you know how. This book will get you to the top when you use it well and keep using it well.

B.R.A.N.D. is the only name you need to know on your checklist for success!

To know when to close the deal is indeed a rare skill, yet a simple one to master! Make it your skill and you will improve the life of everyone around you… and in turn improve your own.

Is there more?

A resounding **YES**!

By investing in this book, you will become a **free** member of www.marcorobinson.com, a revolutionary resource in your sales process and career, where you will receive newsletters, be able to ask questions, and get powerful answers. You will join many others who are breaking new records in their own industries because they have read this book and attended Marco's incredible workshops. You will learn how to deal with the most difficult people, handle any objection, sell to small and big companies, and develop your sales skills into those of a winner and champion. (Please refer to the back pages for further details.)

Until then, see you at the **Champions Conference**!

THE PSYCHOLOGY NECESSARY TO CLOSE THE DEAL!

CHAPTER 1

ATTITUDE EQUALS ALTITUDE!

"You can only sell successfully when you have mastered your attitude!"

Y ou know what? You may have read this before, but if your results are in the gutters, you might want to master this first, as it is fundamental to your success!

Your mindset is everything. Eighty percent of your success is about having the correct attitude. You can't suddenly acquire this attitude halfway through your sales presentation! You must have it before you sell. You need to have it all the time. But if you don't have it yet, you had better read this and learn how to change your ineffective state into an empowering one that guarantees profitable results!

Let me ask you a question. Where do your results come from right now? (Well, if you read the introduction to this book, you **MIGHT** have a small clue as to where you learned the existing lessons in your head. Nevertheless, we'll get more into that later.) First and foremost, your **RESULTS** come from your

ACTIONS. But I do hear your question, and that is, "Why do I take a certain action?" Let's look at the full flow chart first, and then I'll elaborate.

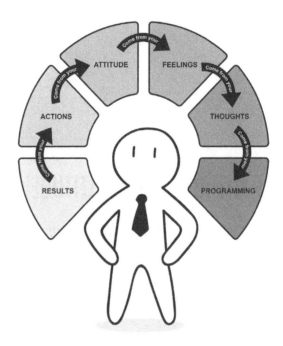

So your results come from your actions, right? Well, of course, what you do creates what you have. It's a simple law of cause and effect. That means what you are doing now is affecting your bank account, because your bank balance is the result of your actions!

What you do, or rather how you do it, comes from your attitude. Your attitude is the way you think. The reason you take action and how you execute that action is from the attitude you have at that time.

You can change your attitude in a heartbeat!

So, if you change your attitude will you get more sales? Yes! But first you must learn where your attitude comes from; otherwise, you won't be able to sustain that new attitude.

How you feel about something will set into action a turn of events. You are either in control of the actions or out of it. Feelings are emotional. Wow, that's news! But seriously, emotion is a very powerful force that can either perpetuate or destroy love. It really is the driving force in everything you do, because all decision-making is based on how you feel.

What do I mean? Well think of it this way: if you have "bad" feelings towards a situation or a person, you won't want to face it or that person, because that would give you emotional and mental pain; it makes you feel lousy on the inside.

For example, if you know someone who regularly makes you feel bad, who always insults you and brings you down, you wouldn't want to spend time with that person, because you feel it'll cost you too much (emotionally and mentally). Later on in this book you will see why it makes sense when you have a difficult customer!

On the other hand, let's say you know somebody who constantly compliments you, listens to what you have to say, and simply makes you feel wonderful. Wouldn't you want to be around such a person more often? Of course you would! You'll be naturally drawn to them because that gives you pleasure! (It's interesting, but all great salespeople are like this.)

Pain and pleasure are the hidden triggers that influence every decision we make, whether we are aware of it or not!

And what's more, interestingly:

We will always do more to avoid pain than to create pleasure.

Let's put all this into perspective. If you really don't feel like making phone calls and telemarketing prospective customers, you just won't do it well. I assure you, every time you manage to get around to it, you know you're going to get the same objections as always. You just don't like it because you are experiencing rejection and rejection is pain! We feel like we are spending time with people who seemingly don't like us. This will create a bad feeling in you. Consequently, a certain attitude towards making phone calls will ensue. You will then take an action that will not be effective and this will get you an ineffective result! You will take an action that will avoid pain but **not** create **growth** in you and your sales!

I hope you're catching on so far and that the results you are getting now are all beginning to make far more sense than they were before! Now here's the kicker:

**There are more connections in the body from the
heart to the head than from the head to the heart!**

So if you're not aware of it, your emotions will dictate your life. You will get up and down results. Your bank account will be cyclical, sometimes good, sometimes bad. If you are very emotional, your bank balance will swing from very good to near bankruptcy, back and forth constantly!

Can you see now that if you don't learn how to control and manage your emotions and channel them in the right way, your results will keep moving up and down like a yo-yo? And I'm sure this is making you an emotional wreck!

So how do you keep your emotions balanced and positive?

Well, firstly, you must realize that all your emotions come from your thoughts.

What you think about the most you will attract the most!

Yes, you've all probably read the "secret" lately and heard of the law of attraction. There is no secret; it's just what you think about. What you focus on will expand! And your results come from what you are thinking now!

So if you are thinking, "I'm not a very good salesperson," you will create that reality and do everything in your power to make that happen! You will not do any prospecting or lead generation. You will do it badly and will not make enough appointments. Furthermore, you will not be enthusiastic and you will not read the rest of this book! Do you know why? Because reading this book will sabotage your belief that says, "I'm not very good salesperson"! Yes, deep down inside, your subconscious mind knows it! If you put anything into your mind that does not serve your negative thought, it will reject it! Quite astounding, isn't it? Yet, it's a fact!

**Your subconscious mind will reject anything
that does not match its programming.**

Are you confused? Good! That means you're about to learn something extremely valuable, and possibly if you're really blessed, life changing!

The most important question here is, "Where the hell are your thoughts coming from? Why are you thinking 'I am not a good salesperson?'"

Your thoughts are coming from your programming. Yes, that means there are programmers "typing into your mind's hard drive," telling you what to do and when to do it. They are programming into you a syntax of words.

What does SYNTAX mean?

**Syntax is the order of your programming down
to the last word and the exact order of those words!**

If you've ever messed around with computers in your life, even just installing a new game, you'll have come across the words **syntax error**.

That, my friends, is not a load of rubbish. It is actually the computer rejecting a command because it simply does not make sense in its existing programming. Therefore it will be rejected until it does make sense. That means the **master program** must change and the **master programmer** must be the one to do it. So you take it back to the shop! (This happens a lot, doesn't it, for those of you who own a computer?)

So who's been programming you?

If you can't answer this question yet, go back to the beginning of this book and you will know.

In a nutshell, from birth, you couldn't choose your parents or your teachers, you didn't have Zig Ziglar motivating you. And because you couldn't choose and you didn't know you wanted to do sales or that you could be financially free through sales, you weren't in control and there was absolutely nothing you could have done about it then. So they (I will refer to them as your environment at the time including your parents and teachers) had a major influence on your life and helped create your existing default program.

Now, if your parents or teachers were not super salespeople and millionaires, chances are, they could not have helped you create the correct program to enable you to reach the success that you want!

Don't blame them though! Then you become a **victim** and start whining about your circumstances. As soon as you blame others for your lack of success, you give away your power to succeed forever!

It wasn't their fault. They learned how to program you from their parents and teachers! They didn't know any better. And besides, since your parents have put up with your crap for so long, make them proud—be successful, make money, and then you can teach them!… Or, you could watch them wither away into vegetables in a horrible retirement home!

You have the power to change your programming. Sadly, most people don't realize this until they're just about to go six feet under!

You are your own master programmer.

You are in control of everything that comes in and out of your mind. You are in full control of the results even if they seem useless. Choosing the victim's life will bring you despair. Change the program and take the heroic journey to paradise!

Heroic journey? Yes, **heroic journey**! No, it doesn't mean you have to jump out of airplanes with no parachute. It just means there's a learning process that's universal in life. That process is: **you must know your existing mindset/ paradigm will not create the result you want** then you must **unlearn** that **ineffective paradigm** and then learn new ways that are effective to create the desired results that you really want.

Now many people will have a lot of difficulty with what I've just said, because somewhere in their mind, something wants to hold on to the past for a sense of certainty, security, and attachment. Most people don't like change because familiarity is safe! The only problem with that as a salesperson is that your results will also remain the same!

So how do you learn what you need and how do you take the heroic journey with ease?

Well, that's why I took the time and trouble to spend three years of my life to work out a road-map for you! And it's really easy! Wouldn't it be fantastic to learn this in the next chapter?

If you said "No," please put this book back on the shelf and come back when you're ready!

Because the fundamental part of learning is you must be ready to learn!

The teacher only appears when the student is ready.

So let's crack on and master the learning process in Chapter 2!

Now if you're like me, you're probably going to skip to Part II to get the sexiest juicy strategies and techniques that you've ever seen. But just remember, you won't be able to execute anything new until you know how to master it and mastering comes from the inside. It makes a phenomenal difference to be able to say something on the outside with total confidence and mean it. This is something which I learned from Anthony Robbins who is a master of communication: "In any communication between two people, it is the one with the most certainty who will always influence the other."

Let's think about that for a moment. Don't you always trust people who have total faith in what they are doing and are able to communicate that? Of course, we don't want to make a mistake, do we? We want to buy from a source of success. People who have mastered themselves and their product or service become successful because they've taken the time to learn how too.

And that learning generates a new paradigm which creates a new faith in what you are doing and that True faith always shows up whenever it is challenged by a doubt or an objection.

That means, when you have mastered your craft, it doesn't matter what the customer says. If they are the right target market, they will have real benefit. If they want to buy what you are offering, they will buy. This is because you have all the answers, you have communicated them with total conviction, and you have become a new resource for them. You have become a **champion closer**.

CHAPTER 2

THE LEARNING PROCESS

"Hyperdrive your way to a Champion Closer's mindset"

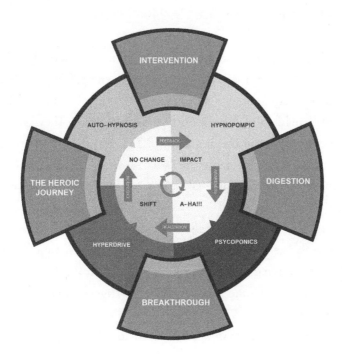

n the previous chapter, I shared that if you keep doing the same things you'll get the same results. This is the stage in your life which I refer to as: **autohypnosis.**

Your present actions are the result of your programming, and eventually when you repeat an action long enough, it becomes habitual and hypnotic in its execution. You have learned the action so well that it has become a part of who you are today. This is your existing **paradigm**.

A paradigm is your exact blueprint and "way" of doing things no matter what. That means you will do things in a certain way if there is no intervention that stops you from doing things that way. What do I mean?

You probably remember "9-11" and the tragic sight of two airplanes hitting the World Trade Center in New York. I remember exactly where I was, who I was with, what time it was at night in my part of the world, and what I was drinking because it was such a **significant**, mind-stopping event. I just couldn't believe it until it was repeated many times on TV.

What you may not be aware of is that around that same time, there were two other airplanes that had also been hijacked, the last of which was Flight 93.

Now let's get a basic paradigm about flying on commercial airlines out of the way. Before 9-11, if an airplane got hijacked, the passengers believed that there would be a very good chance of escaping as they would usually be taken to a deserted airfield and a negotiation would take place. They knew they had a chance of coming out of the ordeal alive. That was the paradigm. However, as soon as those two planes hit the WTC towers, the paradigm suddenly changed globally. A devastating realization was forced upon everyone around the world.

The passengers on Flight 93 also got news that the two other planes crashed and everyone was dead. Before this discovery, they thought they had a good chance of surviving. This news shook them and it motivated them to take a combined action to try and avoid death. (The trigger to avoid pain here had crossed the threshold!)

A fair majority of the passengers decided to take the plane and sabotage the hijackers!

Why? Because they knew they had nothing to lose. They understood that if they didn't do anything they would die anyway, crashed into a building somewhere, killing many others.

At least by trying to take the hijackers they knew they had a chance. At that moment they changed their **paradigm** and took a completely different action from what they would have normally. This action saved thousands of lives as it diverted their aeroplane into a field and not a building. Unfortunately it was not enough to save their own lives. But they live on as some of the bravest people the world has ever known.

They took the **heroic journey** because it made complete sense. And they set a precedent—they scared the hijackers. Had they known sooner the hijackers' plans, who knows, they might have had enough time to save their own lives!

My intention is not to upset anyone with the above event. It is to show that even as an average salesperson, you can do better and achieve far better results by realizing what you are doing right now is creating your future.

If you keep getting the same results over the next five years, how is that going to affect your life? Is that what you really want? Because if you do the same things that's what you will attract—the same dismal results!

To get the best **feedback** from your present actions, just project yourself in the future and see how it'll affect you.

Successful selling and closing is an exact science and is beautiful to look at.

The science is in this book and you need to learn before you improve.

When I was 21 years old, I started my first job as a direct sales person selling timeshare in Spain from an office in Manchester on commission only. And I can tell you it scared the hell out of me for a while because I didn't get any sales!

In fact, for four weeks I had no sales and consequently no money. It was that bad. I had to walk home to my bedsit seven days on the trot and eat a can of processed peas every night because I just didn't have the money.

Now most people would think I was crazy for doing that. But do you know what? I thank God that I had that experience so soon in life! I literally learned through **struggle** to **breakthrough** to success! And I consider myself extremely lucky because I was able to attract into my life a person at that time who gave me a book and said, "Read it, and don't stop reading it, and then read it again!"

That was the **intervention** I needed. And as soon as could, I ran to the office and sold my first two deals, totaling about 20,000 pounds and received 2,000 pounds in commissions! I became salesperson of the month, salesperson of the year, and eventually ended up running the sales and marketing team of the whole country. I did that in the space of three years.

This is not about bragging. You have got to know something about me. You must **know** that I achieved phenomenal success in sales. Otherwise, I wouldn't be qualified to write this book! And you have a great opportunity to learn from someone who has maybe achieved the results that you want. So right now when you are reading this, you are opening your subconscious mind to the intervention that could change your life, your results, and your bank account!

There are other people out there who have achieved greater success than me, oh yes, and I would advise you to also read their writings. In fact, I'm listing a number of books you must read at the end of this book.

However, you will have enough **intervention** in this book to achieve great success. Just read it! Keep reading it and read it again!

Let's begin your learning process.

1. Feedback

This is when you become aware that your existing results are not making you happy and fulfilled now, and more so in the future.

> **Do you know what? This is a fantastic state to be in, because**
> **you've just realized that if you don't change, nothing else will!**

For a change to take effect, you must receive the correct intervention. And this is how the law of attraction works so well. Remember, what you focus on will expand! If you read back a few paragraphs, you'll note that I received intervention from an unlikely source because I was looking for it! I was asking myself desperately every single day this question:

How do I succeed?

I kept asking this question again and again and again. It got louder and louder the more I had to walk home and eat peas—not that I'm suggesting that you eat peas, but that pain was growing. I was being triggered or motivated to take an action. But funnily enough, it wasn't to give in, to quit, because I knew that if I gave up, I would be in a worse position, with even more pain. I knew quitting wouldn't fulfill me, as that wouldn't match the vision in my head of driving a lovely black sports car, going out with a beautiful, classy lady, or making lots of money.

I knew I couldn't go back, literally, I would've rather died, because if you are not able to live your dreams, what's the point of living!

Many years later, I learned that to have success, we must cut off every other possibility except the one we truly want to succeed in. I couldn't conceptualize that then, but in essence, that was what I was doing when I was walking home seven miles a day and eating peas!

2. Intervention

The intervention will only come when you are looking for it. The answer to my question, "How do I succeed," came to me through a senior colleague. I was given a self-improvement book by a top performing salesperson in my company, and it literally changed my life overnight. That guy, who's called Rob by the way, ended up becoming a lifelong friend. I was able to return the favor to him many years later, and let me tell you, it was a great pleasure when I was finally able to do so.

Remember, the teacher will only appear when the student is ready to learn!

Knowing when to close the deal is all about knowing when your customer is ready to buy your offering, and this book will teach you just that—if you read it, keep reading it, and read it again!

If you've bought this book and you're still reading it, you've reached an awesome level of consciousness because you're about to change your bank account in a big way.

You see, you really have to be extremely unhappy with your present circumstances to have the motivation to change them.

**The happy oyster with nothing to irritate it
is not the oyster that produces the pearl.**

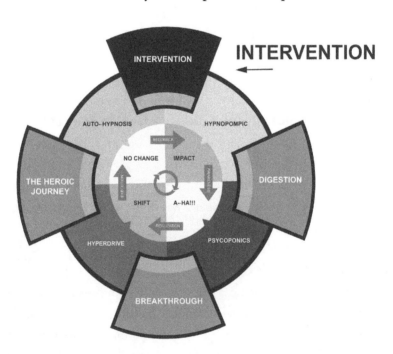

3. Impact

Intervention can be very sudden or it can last many years. However, the more intervention you can get on a sustained level the more growth and better results you'll achieve. Let me explain why.

When I was learning how to sell, my sales managers would always take over at the end of my presentation and attempt to close the customer after they had agreed on a price. Now, normally they didn't get to a price because I hadn't sold anything. This was when I was pea eating!

However, when I was aware and receiving my intervention, my sales improved in the sense that I was able to create more desire for the product I was offering. Consequently, my sales managers stayed longer on my table because they had more interest and could "sniff" a deal. When they stayed longer on the table, I learned everything I needed to learn about how to be successful in sales.

I learned they never took the first no.

In fact, during my first sale, I was completely astounded that the sales manager received over twenty no's from the customer before suddenly the customer changed his mind and said, "Yes"! It wasn't because the customer was forced or manipulated; it was because the sales manager had more experience than me and was able to get the customer to clearly see the benefits of how it could improve their life a lot.

I couldn't believe that. It just shocked the hell out of me, in a good way of course. But I just didn't understand what was happening on the table and why suddenly they said yes!

Of course, now I do know. But at that time, that first time, I realized I was in a **hypnopompic** state.

I'm not using big words to impress you. I'm using this word because I feel it best describes the state we're in when we are shocked! The dictionary defines it as 'the state you are in just before waking up'.

This is an awesome part of your learning process because, to truly learn something, it must impact you on a subconscious level, be disassembled in your mind, and put back together again so it makes sense!

There will be confusion before you learn anything.

Confusion just means it doesn't make sense to your existing mindset. But to perform at a different level, you have to think in a different way!

When you realize this, it's really simple. But for so many people who can't grasp this simple concept, they end up believing that confusion is their mind's way—or God's way—of telling them they can't do something, i.e. "Don't waste your time" and "This is not for you"!

Have you ever heard someone saying, "The reason I didn't succeed was because I realized it just wasn't for me"?

Now when people say this to you, a few things are happening in their mind. First of all, they are justifying the existence and survival of their existing mindset. Their existing mindset isn't ready for growth or change yet because it doesn't want to give up its sense of security. It is also saying they have no clear goals. Why do I say that? Because if you have clear goals in life, you realize that you have to take a different action to achieve your goals. Most people don't know what action to take and don't achieve their goals because they don't have the right intervention.

They don't have the right intervention because they're not asking the right questions in their mind, e.g., **how do I succeed?** Instead of that, they ask questions like:

- Why am I doing this?
- Am I ever going to make more money?
- Why it so hard?
- There must be an easier job!
- Is this really for me?
- Why can't I get any appointments?
- Why can't I close people?

Do you notice any difference in these questions from mine? What's the **pattern** here? Let me explain. Believe it or not, the questions above are emotion-based. They are coming from a place of insecurity; they are coming from a source of a lack of confidence. If you say to yourself, "Why can't I do this," your mind will come back with a direct answer, and the answer will be: "Because you don't know what you're doing!"

Now, here's the kicker. When you get the kind of answer like the one above, how will it affect your self-esteem and confidence to do things as a person? Do you think it'll make you take positive action or do you think you'll feel crappy and worthless?

What will you be doing when you feel so bad about yourself? Well, if you don't have a mentor around to support your growth, you'll absolutely not want to carry on feeling like that, because there's too much pain associated with that kind of low self-esteem. And to avoid prolonging that pain you will find a reason not to continue feeling like that. You will validate and justify your decision by saying, "You know what, this just isn't for me!"

That will make you feel better, won't it? You're absolutely right! You would have just given yourself a dose of morphine, a shot in the arm to make you feel "better". You would have just taken the drug of mediocrity, or sorry, the drug of following the wandering majority. Yes, by quitting and therefore getting a quick-fix for your pain, you would've done what most people do, you know, be happy with your lot, don't complain, just be happy with your $1,000 per month income, etc.

This is called **being average**! There's no pain in just being average. It's really easy to be average. Mediocrity doesn't take much effort.

I know what you're thinking. You thought you had bought a book on how and when to close the deal, right? Of course, and you have! And you'll be very pleased with your results. That's why in the second half of this book I'm showing you every fantastic strategy for getting the results of your dreams, guaranteed to work—when you apply them!

What I didn't tell you earlier was that you'll have to change the way you think, completely, before those results kick in. You cannot have one without the other.

You cannot have success without a mindset that allows you to!

If you have only achieved average results, it means you have a mindset at present that only allows you average results! There's no way on God's earth you're going to drop lucky and achieve phenomenal success if you keep thinking the same way. That's just flat out impossible.

Are you still Hypnopompic? Just testing! I had to say that just in case you didn't get it the first time around!

You see, if your mind cannot find the support it needs through correct intervention on a sustainable basis, it will snap back into autohypnosis, reverting to its PREVIOUS default system.

Can you imagine how often this happens to individuals all over the world every day?

Let's put this into perspective.

Probably one of the greatest golfer's there ever was (and maybe again, IF he can replace his Dad's phenomenal mentoring) was Tiger Woods, because he achieved phenomenal success at such a young age. Did you know that Tiger Woods's father, Earl, used to take him golfing when he was only five years old, every day?

What do you think would have happened if Earl had decided not to take Tiger golfing just because all the best golfers (during those years) were white guys, and that he thought Tiger would never be good enough to compete at international levels? Do you think that might have changed Tiger's entry into the golfing world?

You and I know there would be no way Tiger Woods could have achieved all he has without his father coaching and mentoring him from a very early age. It just couldn't have happened. What happened when his Dad died? Tiger lost his mentor, and subsequently he lost his habit of winning, he literally went off the rails... so now you know it's not just a one off intervention that guarantees consistent success, but a constant input of relevant mentoring!

There was something **driving** Tiger's father, something more powerful than those negative thoughts he could have had. He wanted to create a better future for Tiger than the life he had when fighting in Vietnam. He wanted to avoid that pain and live a far better life through his son. And he knew he had nothing to lose! So he pushed on and motivated his son to practice, practice again, and keep practicing.

Now again, I know what some of you are thinking. "Yeah, Tiger had a great dad. I never had that kind of help from my parents, so I won't achieve the same success! It's just not going to happen, it's too late!"

Only people with a limited mindset would think like that. Thomas Edison was 57 when he finally succeeded with the light bulb—and his dad didn't even know what a light bulb was!

The most successful people in the world didn't have parents who were mega successful before. They just had the right intervention and they saw a future they did not want and decided to change it! In fact, their parents "helped" them see that! Be very grateful when you have that vision!

Joe Gerard is in the Guinness Book of Records for being the best salesperson in the world. He was already almost 50 when he achieved that record! What made him change? He had some serious intervention!

Joe was a car salesman and he was lucky if he sold one car a month. He could barely support his family and three kids, and one day it all got too much for him. One night as the family was dining in their small house there was a very loud knock at the door that just wouldn't stop. His wife answered, and two very big guys walked in, waving a red letter, claiming they were bailiffs and were there to remove all assets from the house.

They even took the TV while his youngest was watching it. The whole family cried and cried and his kids, with tears in their eyes, asked their dad if they were going to have to live on the street.

At that moment, Joe had an incredible realization that if he didn't do something they would be destitute. At first he was hypnopompic. But after digesting this very real nightmare, he told his family with absolute confidence, that in three months they would be living in a house with a swimming pool— and he believed it! Why? Because, he had nothing to lose. He was willing to take responsibility and take the heroic journey and save his family.

The next day, he walked into work and sold 12 cars in one day! Not only did he do that, he sold 12 cars every day for four years to break the world record!

Did he regret the bailiffs turning up at his home that fateful night? Absolutely not! He saw it as a blessing in disguise. For without that pain trigger, he might not have taken the necessary action to change his life and become very rich through sales.

He suddenly grew rich, and, yes, you too can
be very rich through sales, very rich indeed!

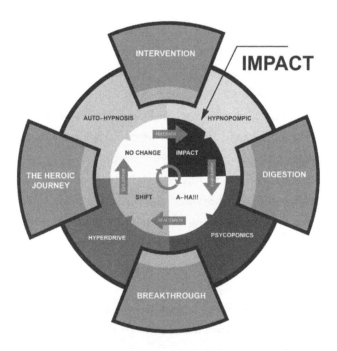

What Joe did was suddenly create a **goal** for himself and took the necessary action to get there. He watched and studied the best salespeople in his company, he read books, he worked very hard, and he got there in a very short time. Shorter than you would ever think.

So once you are hit with something, it will impact you. Sometimes it can be very profound like in Joe's case. But it's what you do with this impact that makes the difference. It's how you digest and process the information that leads to a decision whether it's worth going on and learning how to grow your results, or just snapping back into your comfort zone.

4. Digestion

It is this digestion that will be the key process in determining your future and consequently your results, because you have created a new awareness. Your conscious mind will reason with your subconscious. Sometimes it'll be a wrestling match, sometimes it'll make sense instantly.

In this process, your mind will work out what the cost is compared to the benefits. Your conscious reasoning mind will give you objections to changing, while your subconscious mind will give you the "sight" of seeing what will happen if you decide to take the journey and succeed. If you can't see the benefits, you won't make the necessary changes.

**Remember, people make decisions based
on how they feel, not how logical it is.**

Your subconscious mind is emotional in nature. It "sees" the past, the present, and the future, and sees them through pictures not words. This, as Mr. Spock will say, is not logical! But that's how the mind works. You only do something because you have already "seen" it. So if your conscious mind will not allow you to see what would happen if you took a certain path, you won't do it. This is because your programming has a filter and it filters out anything that does not match that programming. Your conscious mind truly has to see: it has to see the benefits, the **whys**, and the reasons to make such a change in life. Once you have allowed yourself to see this, you can program your subconscious to take the necessary steps to execute your new vision.

**Your vision must be clear, and it must be
supported on the inside and the outside.**

You can only focus on something if it is clear—then you can hit your target. Far too many people walk around with fuzzy targets. They even keep changing their goals because they don't fully believe they'll get there.

All this talk about the mind will make complete sense later in this book, because you have to take your customer through the same learning process to see the benefits of buying your product.

You must know the perfect questions to ask to get your
customer to see the benefits of using your service or product.

The salesperson who doesn't realize the statement above will always be average and never understand why they can't improve.

This is a huge step in realizing your dreams. You'll have to master creating a picture your customer can relate to; you'll have to paint the picture for them. Every brush stroke will determine your success or failure.

People won't buy anything if they can't see the benefits of using it quickly and clearly.

"What a fool cannot see he will laugh at."—Anon

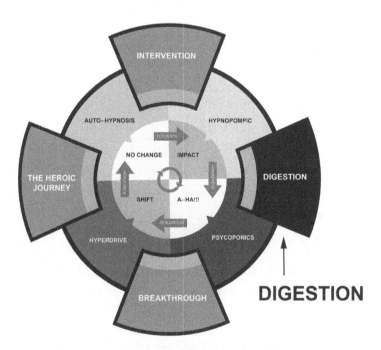

Therefore, you must have first seen for yourself the customer benefiting in your mind. To see this, you must first believe it! You can only **transfer belief** when you already have it yourself. Selling is all about that transference of belief!

The little teaching I was doing above is putting you into the next phase of the learning process.

5. Psychoponics

Let me ask you a question. If I asked you what would be the best place to learn how to achieve fantastic sales, what would you say?

Before you answer, I can tell you, the best place to learn how to achieve fantastic results is to have a fantastic learning environment, or the most **fertile environment** possible that allows you to grow the quickest and most powerful.

Psychoponics is the place for that, and before you ask, this word is not in the dictionary. It was coined by a very clever and successful friend of mine, Paul Counsel, to describe the best place to learn.

It is taken from the word "hydroponics", which is the most fertile place plants can grow to their full potential because that environment contains the most nutrients plants can uptake in the fastest possible time.

Psychoponics is growing your mind in the most fertile way to give you the necessary tools to get out there and make it happen in the quickest possible time!

In the second half of this book, you'll be immersed in psychoponics again, again and again if you read this book, read it once more, and then read it again and again. This book is a fertile learning environment that will give you tremendous support through your growth. It is your companion, your guide, and it should never leave your side if you want to be seriously rich from sales and deal-making.

One of the most important parts of psychoponics is learning that mistakes are good, meaning you have to make mistakes to learn another way of doing something. Whenever you learn something new, it'll be like an alien in your system. It'll be strange and not "belong" to you until you start using it again and again.

You must repeat something without the fear of messing up before you get it right. That means, you must know how not to do it first! You must **eliminate** what doesn't work!

Thomas Edison had to make 10,000 mistakes before he got it right. And even then the light bulb only came on for a split second and burned out. He had to make thousands of more **mistakes** to eliminate what wouldn't work.

**That takes great faith and courage, two of the
attributes you must have to get rich from scratch.**

You have to learn that you will not get it right at first, because you have spent years and years learning how to get an average result very well! In fact, your skills at being average far surpass your skills at being successful because you have been doing it for so long and there are so many other people doing it, so you feel connected in your averageness. You are not lonely!

You are so good at getting what you don't want because you focus on it all the time! Saying to yourself, "I don't want more bills," will bring you more bills! Saying, "I don't want another 'I'll think about it' objection," will bring thousands of those objections, because that's all you are thinking about!

What you should be asking is:

"How do I succeed and overcome the 'think about' objection?"

Do you think that will change your focus? Do you think you'll get answers? Of course, because now you're asking the right questions! Incidentally, learning how to ask your customers the right questions is a big part of psychoponics.

If you called me and said, "Listen, Marco, I don't want to get more objections," I'll tell you, "Guess what, you are going to get thousands more—more than you've ever imagined possible!"

You see, what many average deal-makers don't know is that the more objections you get, the more sales you get, because an objection is a sign that the customer is seriously considering your offer: they are having a logical-emotional debate in their minds and their emotion is beginning to see something valuable.

**In essence, if you don't get any objections, you won't
be getting any sales, because your customer is not
focused on your product. They're just not serious!**

Now, this might be a steep learning curve for you, but what you've just learned is extremely useful. Instead of being frightened of objections, you're going to learn to welcome as many objections as you can get!

Now isn't that a **new paradigm**? It gets much better, just hold onto your seats, because you're going to learn to enjoy asking for objections. Yes, you're going to love asking, "What are your objections to buying this today?"

Why are you going to love this? Because you'll learn it is the most effective way of destroying the objection and giving your customers more reasons to buy what you are offering!

We'll talk more about this later, but I guarantee, if you are willing to learn from me and focus, you will love every objection coming to you! Because you will soon discover it leads to more money in your bank account!

Mistakes are crucial to success and you can't have success without failure. Take soccer for example. The best players in the world focus on getting the ball into the back of the net for ninety minutes and fail most of the time. Nowadays, the coverage of matches is so advanced that it'll even tell you on the screen how many attempts there have been on scoring and how many successes.

Goal scorers are just **great closers**, but they know a close doesn't come without an opening! We'll also cover this later.

A goal doesn't come without a goal-scoring opportunity!

And **gratitude** is a huge part of moving through your learning process. If you are **bitter** about your circumstances, you cannot move forward because you're taking the role of a victim and are stuck in the past. Victims will always be left behind because they spend all their energy blaming everything apart from themselves. Victims don't take responsibility!

Learning can only take place when you accept your circumstances and take full responsibility for them. You are the master programmer. The reason you are where you are today is because you have programmed yourself to be who you are.

**You only learn by doing what you have
learned and what you are learning!**

So the last part of the learning process is perfecting your new skill. But most significantly, realizing you can do it. Ironically, though, you can only realize it when you are doing it!

6. Shift

The shift in your belief system will follow immediately after you realize you can do it. This realization occurs only after you have spent enough time in psychoponics.

This paradigm shift is always an **a-ha** moment, something that "clicks" within you suddenly. It is a shift which will change your consciousness and how you think forever. From then on, you will follow a different path than that which you have taken before. You will tread on a new highway of different outcomes— those that you have desired and previously dreamed about, and you'll look back at the old path and say to yourself, "Why the hell did I stay on that path for so long?" Then a realization will come upon you: that that path was a blessing because it led you to where you are going now. You will become very **grateful** for where you are now.

The a-ha moment is when you finally "get it", meaning you have gained a full understanding of what you have learned. This is the shift in your mindset— and this is when you hit **hyperdrive**.

Why? Because you can now do what you have learned and it works and you get a different result! That means your **feedback** gives you a positive change and the results **reinforce** that change. It gives you **exponential growth** from the root of your mindset.

In fact, when you get an a-ha moment, you kind of forget your past and you just keep moving forward. It's like solving a clue in a crossword puzzle (if you enjoy playing games) or when eventually you learn how to drive a car or whatever new skill you are focused on.

It is only when you have the a-ha that you gain confidence and are able to execute what you have learned. And you know what? It'll feel really good, and when it feels good, you'll feel good every time you do it! You will enjoy doing it. In fact, now it'll actually take less energy and yet, automatically, you'll get a completely different outcome!

Michael Jordan was an awful basketball player when he was in high school. He was so bad he got thrown off the school team because he just couldn't get it together on the court. Was he miserable? Absolutely. He cried and punished himself. He became a real victim. And one day, when all the emotions had subsided, he realized he just wasn't good enough.

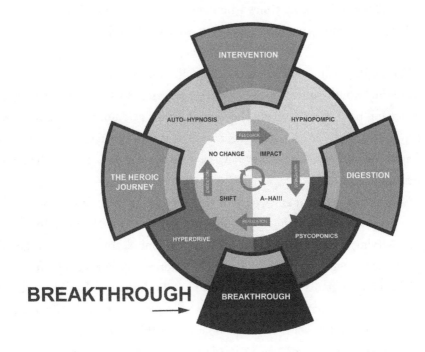

So what did he do? He went to his dad for help. His dad asked him if he was serious, and Michael answered he would do anything to get back on the team. His dad told him to prove it!

So Michael got up at 5:00 a.m. every day and started "practicing", meaning repeating his mistakes again and again, and then changing the way he did things. Through the process of elimination he "found his game", and he kept repeating the same moves not just a few times, but literally thousands of times.

His a-ha moment came when he finally understood he had to learn through mistakes and if he kept practicing he would get better and better. Was his mind in doubt? Yes, of course, but the pain of not being on the team motivated him to focus and push through the challenges.

That decision made him the best player in the world for many years. It wasn't talent that got Michael Jordan there. It was **focus** that made him outstanding! And focus is the determining factor in winning at sales.

There'll be many times when you will doubt, but sticking to your game and repeating what works will work.

One of the main reasons successful people rise from absolutely nowhere is because they would rather face the challenge of learning what they needed to do than staying poor all their lives. They know if they give up, they might as well not live. This inner drive pushes them, and they take the heroic journey again and again because they know they have to learn to be different than where they came from!

Change the program and you will change your bank account. You are the master programmer. Load the right programs. Throw out the old programs—they are not serving the success you want. Read this book, learn the new programs, and key them in again and again. This will reinforce your new paradigm.

Your new programs will be delivered to you in the second half of this book. They are winning programs and have never failed to achieve a fantastic outcome for me and many thousands of people on a sustainable basis.

Can they be improved? Maybe, but I've yet to see anything that works better than what you'll see here and I keep updating when I find an improvement. I'll tell you about them in my newsletters, which you'll get on a regular basis to reinforce your psychoponics.

I believe in constant learning, not analyzing. If you start analyzing what you are learning here, you'll lose the whole structure. Some people try to do that, but it's like leaving the tomatoes out of the tomato soup! It just won't taste the same.

And you know what? If you start tinkering you're not going get the result you want. You'd be messing with 20 years of practice. You can learn to be better from people who are getting far better results, instead of analyzing and tinkering the lessons. Trust them and you will fly!

So what's the best way to practice?

**Role play, do it, role play, do it, role play,
role play, role play some more, and do it!**

I've discovered that if you did something seven times by actually repeating it exactly, you will retain 67 percent of the information you need to learn. So what happens if you repeat 2,000 times? You'll get better and better, obviously! You'll be creating new neural pathways in your mind that will empower your success! You'll have a new blueprint!

However, you won't create a more powerful mindset if you read this book only once. You will retain your old program and you'll continue with your current result.

Now I have been repeating myself many times in this book so far and I will keep repeating myself, not because I'm trying to bore the hell out of you, but because you need to see it again and again. Your subconscious needs to be impressed that this is the blueprint. All blueprints have designs, and you need to draw the design and make it permanent in your head so that you can't rub it out and go back to square one! This by the way is what most people do, because they don't know the **law of repetition**.

The Law of Repetition will get you there in the fastest possible manner. It is the fastest way to grow, the fastest way to succeed. It is the fastest way to never have money problems again! Will it be easy and comfortable? No. Will it be convenient? No. But it is the fastest way possible.

Hyperdrive will be the speed of your learning. Hyperdrive is the fastest way to travel from point A to point B. Look at how an engine works: the pistons move up and down the same way all the time, but the more you concentrate and press the pedal, the faster you get there!

Press down the gas pedal when you have realized your new skills. Test them again and again, and please don't make the excuse that you've got no one to practice on. You talk to yourself, don't you? I know you do—everyone does, except I do it out aloud, and people look at me weird sometimes. But guess what? They are not in charge of my life, I am! So don't worry about what other people think! It doesn't matter because they are not you, and you have to learn to disassociate from people who don't support your growth, otherwise they will drag you down into their world and you will get their results! That's a big mistake some people never learn from. Sorry, but I have no sympathy for those people who look at me weird because they have a disease.

It's called poverty! Stay the hell away from such people!
Their disease is highly contagious if you get too close!

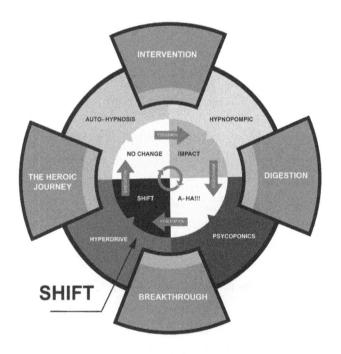

7. The Heroic Journey

Victims don't take journeys. They just stay in the same place in the same pattern, griping and moaning about how unfortunate they are and it's not their fault. The simple fact is they don't take responsibility for their actions. They blame other people and circumstances.

It's sad to know how common this is since conventional education just doesn't give us the best platform to be rich. It confines us and limits our imagination. Imagination is the genius behind success. Einstein accredited it to all his breakthroughs.

Heroes, however, are always willing to take the journey because they have courage. Courage is not the absence of fear; it is doing what you have to do despite the fear. You will experience fear along your heroic journey, along your learning process, but it will only disappear when you keep doing what you're afraid of! **When you master what you are learning.**

All salespeople are afraid of rejection. If they say they aren't, they are lying to you. Every salesperson would love to close every client. However, you're going meet prospects with no credit card, no job, and problems, i.e. people who are just not ready or suitable for your offering. Meaning, they are not going to benefit. It would be wrong to sell to them and you will know it because it will feel wrong. What should you do then? Just do what you have learned and ask for referrals even if they don't buy. Now, they will only give referrals if you have given them everything you've got and your best shot, which they will respect. That will make them "see" some of their friends benefiting from what you've got.

The heroic journey is understanding that rejection is part of the game and part of the process and you have to go through it again and again to achieve success. It is a **numbers game** that equates to: the more qualified people you see, the more sales you will get.

"Qualified" means people whom you know can benefit, because you have seen them benefiting, they have the disposable income to afford your offering, and will use your product or service to improve their lives.

We shall talk about qualifying later. Effective qualifying will save you a lot of time hunting for the "gold" clients than sifting through lots of unqualified people. Chasing unqualified prospects around will waste their time and yours—and they won't thank you for it!

Champion salespeople know they are not going close everybody and that rejections are not an emotional "get at them" from their prospects. The prospects are in fact secretly telling you how not to sell to them!

If you take rejection personally, your self-esteem will drop like Enron shares when the corruption was revealed. Heroes wear a force-field that cannot be penetrated by even the most negative person. Any attack will simply be deflected. Heroes will remain invincible in their mindset and raise their game even more. In fact they will use it to rally themselves to a stronger position and repeat their presentation.

Heroes don't give up until the job is done and the customer is rescued into a far better lifestyle because of your product or service!

A fantastic example of this is the Rocky film series and how it echoed Sylvester Stallone's life in getting the picture made. Rocky just wouldn't give up. He just kept going until he eventually beat Apollo Creed in Rocky II. This is the kind of strength which people absolutely connect with and love. It may give you goose-bumps, but that is what the entire Hollywood film industry is based on: the victim to hero story. I personally don't know of many films that don't have this element, and that's why they are so successful, again and again!

Even more remarkable is how Stallone won the Oscar for Best Film from seemingly nowhere. Just 12 months before, he was completely broke, had no job and no prospects, and was living in a dump. He even had to sell his dog to eat. But one night after repeating and repeating, for the umpteenth time,

How can I be successful?

Stallone got his answer! After watching a documentary on the famous Rocky Marciano, he wrote the script for Rocky in one night!

Did he get the film made? No, they all rejected him, every studio until one offered him $ 25,000 to make it. But he said no. Why? Because the condition was he had to star in it. He wanted to be the main lead in the film even though he had zero acting credibility. The studio owners laughed and offered him more money. He still said no, and they kept going up until they eventually agreed on a deal. And the rest, as they say, is history!

If you want to know the full story—and I highly recommend that you listen to it—go online to "YouTube" and search for Anthony Robbins and he'll tell this amazing story in the best way that I've heard it. It is truly inspiring.

Stallone took the journey and kept going and kept accepting rejection and using it to learn and grow. Heroes make things happen, while victims just wonder what the hell happened!

The next part of your journey is getting out there and doing what you have learned again and again. You will get the results!

The reason I wrote this book is to show you that it is very easy once you've got the training! It becomes a part of who you are, a habitual way of doing things. In fact, you will do it so well that you won't even consciously know you're doing it! How come? Because by then:

- You are executing your actions with autohypnosis!
- You have completed the cycle!
- You are operating with a new program and a new default system that will simply not accept average in any way, just outstanding!
- You have raised your standards.

- It is not an effort because you have learned it.
- And you have support from the deepest core of who you as an individual.
- You have grown into someone else, someone you prefer, someone you love!

I know this has been a long chapter, but I must share one last thing with you before we move on, and it's crucial to your success!

Support and Mentoring

Friends, get yourselves in **good company**. I mean hang around with people who support you, your growth, and your journey!

You become who you spend time with the most.

Yes, this may sound weird, but if I were to teach you just one thing from this book, it would be this: change to an environment that assists you!

If there are people around you who don't think the same way as you or doubt your capability to succeed, ditch them! Yes, I mean stop spending time with them because they will cause a paralyzing disease inside you, and you won't be able to start your journey. You will start to question any book you read or any intervention you might receive, because in your other ear, you've got this other person—or worse, other people—telling you to stop wasting time listening to whackos like me and trying to be someone else!

As soon as you listen to that, you are dead. Don't listen to them!

Here's something you may not know. When you start to really **grow**, people notice it. This change in you will stand out like a big, red, flashing light. And some of your "friends" might not like it as they realize they may lose you and then they'll have no one to gripe and whine to! What you don't know is that they are afraid to grow, because growth requires change and some people can't handle change at all.

Success is choosing who you spend your precious time with. If you surrender your programming to another victim, say goodbye to your dreams!

I spent five years with a partner who didn't offer me any growth and limited my bank account, and I ended up having the same problems as him. Yes, it wasn't comfortable splitting. It was a little emotional but everything inside me told me to do it!

My only regret is that I didn't do it sooner. It cost me a lot more money than it should have. But I learned from that mistake and have since spent time with only people who give me growth. Yes, it has been uncomfortable at times because I was less confident while I was learning from them. But by God, I'm making a hundred times more cash than when I was with my partner, and I'm living my dreams every day!

One good decision can revolutionize your income!

Your friends will either move with you or you will leave them behind and I can tell you this: true friends will be there for you in every misfortune and eventuality. They will be there to help you because they care about you. They will actually love your growth and will love to help you through it because they know you would do the same for them! "Friends" who don't show up in times of trouble or who simply disappear when tough times come don't deserve to be called your friends. Just move on and look for other reliable and trustworthy people who will help you through the journey.

The more time you spend with great people, the faster you will grow and succeed. Their success will rub off on your blueprint, and your program will be upgraded continually!

Now some people say to me, "But I don't know anyone like that!" Don't panic, use other ways and means! Read more books that support your growth, read a book a day if you have to! Go to seminars, events, and gatherings—change your environment. Focus on doing these activities. It is very important that you do, because just when you least expect it, you will have your a-ha moment!

The Learning process of the master closer has been illustrated in a Diagram throughout this Chapter… how this whole learning process works, how you go through the cycle. Do refer to it as you reread this book. Copy it into your planner or diary. Look where you are along this learning process, learn from it, go through the cycle. If you can get personally mentored, it'll give you rocket speed growth and success. One-to-one coaching is the most effective way to improve. If you want to know more about this, go to my website www.marcorobinson.com.

CHAPTER 3

THE BUYING PROCESS

"Pin-point your prospects buying cycle to the last second!"

Your customer must learn how to buy your product. Every single prospect you come across will have to go through their own learning—and buying— process before they will subscribe to your offering. The difference this time is that your customer has to learn quickly! And just like your own learning process, they eventually will have a shift in their consciousness and adopt a new paradigm to be "sold" on your presentation.

So how do you do this?

In the "Psychoponics" section (later in this book), you will master all the techniques necessary to persuade your customer to your way of thinking. But first of all, you must understand their buying process.

The legendary philosopher, Aristotle, came up with the acronym, **A.I.D.A.** (Attention—Interest—Desire—Action).

He was a genius, literally way ahead of his time. This strategy has been around forever and is still working. However, I'm going take it a stage further.

In today's world, you have less time to get your prospects' Attention and keep it. In fact, you'll have to make a very good case for them to spend time with you before you're even allowed to present your super amazing product. People are getting smarter and more resistant to incredulous manipulation. They detest being manipulated or feel like they've been scammed—just like you and I. So what do we do?

Since your prospect is very afraid of making a big mistake if they buy your product, you will have to take away this fear before you have a buyer!

To actually make a customer feel secure in their purchase, they will have to have trust in you and what you are offering a lot. They will have to know you are more than a friend.

They have to know you are a resource!

And they have to know you'll be around to support them in their purchase for a long time to come! (Isn't that what you want when you buy something?)

So how does it start? It's really fascinating, and when I learned it, I shouted **A-HA**—many times! The steps of the buying process are:

1. DE-HYPNOTIZE
2. STRATEGIC INTERVENTION
3. ATTENTION
4. CONFUSION
5. AWARENESS
6. SOLD!

Stage 1: De-Hypnotize

Share with them. Earn the right to listen.

Yes, your customers are in **autohypnosis** right now, using the products they have. They will protect their decision to buy whatever they've bought and they will always compare it to yours even if it is related in the smallest of ways. Some people will be so hypnotized and brand hooked that they won't even want to hear what you've got. What they really want to know is—can you help them **do it faster, longer, cheaper, and better and not make a mistake doing so?**

Please note that I did not mention price. Selling something because it is cheaper will eventually kill you, because at some point, it'll cost more to sell what you've got than the company spent on producing it!

Secondly, if you can't get them to trust you and build rapport, they won't buy it even if they could see the benefits. You would've actually blocked them from buying it! This is a great example of successfully getting your BRAND out their through all the channels necessary, especially and essentially including social media...You cannot use the B.R.A.N.D strategy in the first Chapter of this book if your followers are not sufficiently engaged in what you doing and who you are... **de-hypnotizing** is all about the correct **intervention** and knowing when to do it. The correct intervention is delivered by asking the customer questions about what they are doing now with the product or service they have and how they are managing with it.

Throughout the rest of this book you are going to learn how to ask questions, then learn how to listen. Question & Listen—it's really that simple!

The only way to find out what people want is by asking them—unless you can read minds! You will have to ask them very simply what they like about their existing product and what they don't like, or how they are solving their problem now and how it's working for them.

If from the onset you just start trying to sell them your product and tell them yours is better than theirs, they'll vigorously defend their need to be right in their previous purchase. They don't want to appear foolish! Admitting a "mistake" (especially to a total stranger) is demeaning and lowers their self-esteem. It'll make them feel very insignificant. No. They want to feel important!

Recently, I introduced a very close friend of mine who's a beautician to one of the latest skincare ranges. She wouldn't buy it no matter what I did even though I knew it was far better than what she was using. She wanted to keep using her existing products, as her clients were happy with them. She didn't want to buy mine and risk losing her clients because of it.

So what did I do? I eventually had my a-ha moment and decided to buy her the whole range of skincare, investing my own money! I asked her to try it for one day, and if she didn't like it, she could return it to me without any obligation. Being the friend that she is, she was curious. So she tried it on herself. Then she rang me, literally just a few hours after I had given her the products and said, "Marco, this cleanser is absolutely beautiful! I'm going to try the moisturizers overnight and tomorrow and let you know."

Then, to my surprise, she called back again after another hour and said, "Marco, I've just used the cleanser again, this time on one of my regular clients— and she loves it! In fact, I just sold the whole set to her! Can you order me another one?"

At no time did I force a purchase. I just followed my trained intuition and realized that it would be her clients who would validate her purchase the most. When she was able to please a client, she was overwhelmed and called me straightaway.

Yes, she is a special friend to me, but I still needed her to be sold on the products I gave her to use. That phone call which I received from her, although not fully unexpected, made me feel fantastic. Not because I made loads of money, but because I was able to make a big difference to her life by enhancing her business. And guess what? She now sells more skincare than any other of my friends and customers, and consequently, she has added another revenue stream to her business!

So I felt good, she felt good, the client felt good, and the business improved! That's what I call an awesome product!

Sampling is an awesome strategy if used effectively and at the right time.

Comparing will create a war, sharing will create engagement.

Here's a little example:

Question: How do you solve that problem now in your business?
Answer: Well, I use the PDQ widget breaker and it does this and this. I love it!

Question: Wow, that sounds fantastic! Could you share with me how that actually helps you, I would be very interested!

Answer: Sure, it would be my pleasure. It does it this way…

This dialogue could go on for a while. It's very pleasant. The customer thinks they are helping you and they will feel good about this, so let it continue! The other dynamic that's happening here is you are getting your customer to really share with you the perceived benefits so you are not a threat to them. They begin to feel more important. They are also telling you everything upfront, which actually means they can't really change what they said later in your presentation. This is information gathering. You are finding out what they like!

Then you can change your line of questioning by asking them what they don't like about what they are using now. This will break their pattern and make them suddenly think outside of their autohypnosis. But remember, it is far more effective to ask this question when you have built a solid rapport with them, something which we shall talk about later.

Question: Can I ask you what you don't like about your PDQ, some of the things it doesn't do? Or an even stronger question.

Question: If you could improve three things about your PDQ, what would you change to help you more effectively in your business?

Answer: Errrrmmm… (Don't worry if they hesitate. This is a sign they have never been asked this question before. It is a more thought-provoking question.) Well, I sometimes wish it would do this and this and help me in that area.

You are now leading them and you can only lead them to the better product or service when you have rapport!

Now understand this: if at any time during the conversation above, the prospects feel that you are manipulating them or trying to sell them something, they will raise their defense system. You will know when this happens because they won't want to answer your questions anymore.

Also, if you ever say to them that what they bought earlier was complete crap, they will resent you, and again their defense shields will be raised very quickly! And the response to your earlier question will be, "There's nothing wrong with my product! It can't be improved in any way! It's already perfect!" Yes, that's an emotional response, and they're indirectly telling you they don't like you!

Why do most salespeople get into this situation?
Because they want the sale more than the friend!

While your prospects may be in autohypnosis, they still do have radars, and those radars will pick up on key phrases and words—just like Google search!

You've got to keep below the manipulation radar!

This doesn't mean you're about to attack them. It means every time "you share with them," you listen to their answers, you hang on to every word, you show interest in them, you focus on them. (Yes, sharing includes lots and lots of listening!) This will encourage them to share with you more because you have built more trust. This will inspire them to give you more attention!

Stage 2: Strategic Intervention

Strategic Intervention Facilitates Attention.

What do I mean? Let me share a little story from the movies to help you understand better. I know you may not be a big fan of Star Trek, but I am, so here goes!

In the film, *Star Trek: Generations*, while trying to repair his damaged starship, the Enterprise, Captain Kirk is caught into an energy ribbon called the "Nexus". This ribbon of energy is basically another dimension, in which anything you want or dream about actually comes true. You actually get to live your dream life there.

Fast-forward 75 years, and the captain of the new Enterprise starship is Captain Jean Luc Picard. To make a long, breathtaking story short, while pursuing an insane villain, Captain Picard also gets sucked into the "Nexus"!

Suddenly Picard finds himself in a Christmas day dinner with a ready-made family which he has only dreamed about all these years. All his friends who had died are there to share in the fun. This is his perfect, ideal life, the one which he has dreamt about again and again, and suddenly he has it!

Number one: He is **hypnopompic**.

Number two: He has been given supreme **intervention** which has fulfilled his every want and need.

Number three: It all appears **real**. He can feel and touch it.

Number four: He can see the **benefits**. He is experiencing them.

Number five: He starts to believe it, and he begins to enjoy his new environment. He is happy, but…

Number six: His **logic** starts to question his surroundings. He starts asking questions. He's confused!

Number seven: An old friend appears in front of him, a friend to answer his questions. This friend explains to him that he is in the "Nexus" and anything he dreams, anything he wants will be a reality. He can literally have anything without any effort whatsoever.

Number eight: **A-HA**, he suddenly realizes, "This is not real," and he becomes fully aware! He realizes his mortality has been lost. There is no purpose anymore, no meaning, no connection, no uncertainty. And he doesn't want it!

Number nine: He starts **asking** more questions, like how he can get back and save his starship and those lives taken by the insane villain. His old friend reveals that Captain Kirk is also inside the "Nexus" and may be able to help him!

Picard is shocked, but in another ah-ha moment, he decides to take action and locate Kirk.

He soon finds Kirk, who's also living his dream life in a log cabin by the countryside. But no matter what Picard says to Kirk about helping him save numerous innocent lives, Kirk does not want to know! He's having every need, every want fulfilled all the time—why would he want to leave that kind of a world?

Picard shouts, he pleads, he forces, but Kirk would not budge. He's so happy in his autohypnotic state.

Picard then realizes he has to change his approach.

So how does Picard eventually persuade Kirk to join him? Well, Picard starts to **share** in Kirk's world. He starts cooking with him, riding horses with him, and all kinds of outdoor activities with him.

Picard dives into Kirk's hypnotized state and
starts to see Kirk's viewpoint to understand him.

And guess what happens? Kirk starts to like him! He sees a kindred spirit in Picard. He realizes they shared something very special—they have both captained the Enterprise, they have both been the heroes, they have both saved lives when called upon—they have fulfilled their highest calling!

Kirk suddenly realizes he can't be a hero anymore, because the life he's living now is not real. There's no more adventure. Through this process, Picard starts to intervene and in small ways shares with Kirk what it's really like to captain the Enterprise, how many lives are at stake, that they are the only ones who can save everyone, etc.

And at the right moment Kirk is called to action.

You can only call people to action, i.e. get them to buy from you, when you are fulfilling their need, not yours, and they can see that clearly. You will be a resource to them because you are facilitating a life improvement. That's when you have become the **messenger**, not the salesperson.

**People love messengers in every form,
but only if they bring good news!**

Stage 3: Attention

This word means "taking notice". If we really break it down, if someone is taking notice of you, they are literally "interested" in what you're saying. To me, attention is a better word to describe how people buy from you. Without it, you will never generate interest because they are not looking at you or taking any heed of you at all. What they will be looking at is their phone, the best indicator today, the measure if you have their attention or not!

Okay, we've already talked about the first two stages of the buying process, of getting and earning your prospects' attention. However, if you don't know what to do next, they will very easily fall back to their earlier state of autohypnosis!

Why? Because of this thing called ADD—attention deficit disorder.

Here's something I've believed for a very long time, which was recently confirmed by another coach and lecturer, Rick Shrefner. It is now believed that nearly 75 percent of people suffer from ADD—not just children who are hyperactive, but everyday people like you and me. That's most people!

Here's a little secret about me: I get bored very easily. If I don't find something useful or meaningful to occupy my time, I'll get bored quickly. Then I'll turn on the TV, text a friend, listen to some music, go out, or whatever. I will do almost anything, just so that I don't get bored!

Now that I've said this, you'll probably become aware of other people who are like this. Have you noticed how most people respond to beeps, clicks, and ringtones, like they have been programmed by their own smart phone? Their mind and body are hypnotized by those sounds! If not, why would people read and react to text messages while they were talking to you? Why else would they laugh, frown, or stare and stare at those messages, and then excuse themselves to absorb what those messages were saying and then reply them while they are sitting with you? They do this even while driving!

I'm not sensationalizing this and I'm not exaggerating! Think about the world you are living in now. Some people actually carry two phones around and have learned to text from both at the same time!

Why do you think text messaging is hugely popular? Because it's quick and short, and people love getting messages! Getting a message actually lifts a person's self-esteem. It somehow makes people feel wanted. And you are going to have to deal with many ADD prospects and clients! So you'll have to find a way to retain their attention.

Today's world offers more distractions than ever before—bells, beeps, whistles, tones, tunes, and who knows what. There has never been a time when our time has been so competed for. Even if you did everything right, people still answer their mobile phones and send text messages in the middle of your presentation! You're not going to be able to avoid this. But I'll tell you what, if you allow this to happen, you're not going close many deals.

If someone answers his phone while he's with you, then he's not paying attention to you. He is not focused on you or on what you are saying. That can only mean this: you haven't intervened in their mindset for them to justify switching off their phones. Don't blame them.

**They just have not "seen" the benefit yet
of listening or paying attention to you!**

So, you have to allow them to see the benefits very quickly in the buying cycle, not all of the benefits, just a few. If you do a really good job of this, they will literally tell you, "You know what, I'm just going to make this last call and turn off my phone. I need to listen to this!"

Yes, that's right, they will actually say that. And when it happens be very thankful, because that means a hell of a lot! In fact, in this day and age, it means so much that it's nearly as good as closing the deal! It's very close to that achievement! So yes, if they want to turn off their mobile phones, they are paying attention.

If you want to, you could ask them to turn off their phones before making your presentation. But a lot of people don't like this as it may appear to them that you are trying to take control of them—and it could backfire!

**There has to be a very logical reason why they should
turn off their phone and pay attention to you.**

Indeed a mobile phone these days is an extra limb—without one most people feel completely helpless! It's a massive part of their lives because it keeps them connected to their support system which has a massive influence on their lives and their decision making.

So to keep their attention—and I'll be talking a lot more on this in the "Psychoponics" section of this book, you need to **flash** some of the benefits in front of them for them to keep taking notice!

**You have to reveal something that will get
their attention, and they have to see it.**

Another analogy for you: I'm sure most of you reading this book have been to the cinema before because you wanted to watch a certain movie. But what got you there?

Well, here's an answer. Whenever you watch a movie, they will always put the start time about twenty minutes before the actual feature film. They do this as a strategy to make you watch trailers or **previews** of upcoming **new** movies. This is so they can sell you to keep coming back to watch more movies!

And these previews are never boring. They are jam-packed with all the best possible bits in the film, and they edit it in such a way that you want to know how it turns out! If it's an action movie, they'll show the best explosions, car chases, thrills and spills—everything to get you excited enough to go and see it! If it's a comedy, they'll show you the really funny clips to get your attention and eventually peak your interest.

These trailers will also leave you feeling confused, and that is exactly what they are supposed to do. Confusion leads to frustration, and people usually want to fill that "hole" with what happens next!

"I wonder what happens next?"

Or, in your case, you'll want your prospect to ask,

"I wonder if this product could really help me?"

This is the question your prospects should be asking in their minds. They won't say this out loud; they'll keep that to themselves and will instead disguise this "internal question" as an objection or a buying "interested" clarification question!

For your reference and for your convenience—and because I'm so nice—I'm listing a number of these questions in the "Psychoponics" section for you to match up attention and interest in what you are selling to them. But for now, here are two of the more common ones if they are paying attention. They would sound something like these: "So, how does that work then?" and "Would it be able to do this for me?"

Either one of these questions is telling you they are interested. Well done! They are starting to see a clear benefit.

Now, what's more important is your response after they've asked the above questions. And it should be something like this: "If I could show you that it did fill that widget space and cost you less time, would you be interested in looking at this further and seeing how it could work for you?"

Now, what you're asking your customer is a **closing question**, but know that I would never ask a closing question until I knew when the best time was, and the best time to ask a closing question is when you have their attention and their interest. This is absolutely crucial in winning your customer because more customers will buy from you when you know when to ask the right questions! And please note:

You can only close a customer when you have opened them!

And, when:

You already know their answer!

That means you know the customer will give you a positive answer!

Now I know the customer will answer yes to me because I have engineered the syntax of the question to get a positive response. He effectively already said yes in his own question when he asked, "Would it be able to do this for me?"

The point is, instead of you saying yes, get the customer to say yes! Are you getting this yet? It will be so easy when you know how, but getting the customer to say yes moves them miles closer to buying your offering!

Why?

**Because people believe everything that comes out
of their own mouths, and if they don't, they're liars!**

Remember, you are transferring belief and you have to give the customer every opportunity to believe in the product and in you! This creates trust!

So how do you flash the benefits and keep their attention?

In your de-hypnotizing and sharing stage, you would have found out a lot of information about your prospect's needs and wants. That's why you will be able to intervene at the right time when you've shared with them. So you've got to remember something the prospect wants and keep pressing the hot button.

Let's give this a trial run. Imagine your prospect's hot button is "quality and time saving".

Your flash benefit would be: "If this widget was in your pocket right now, was able to answer your email and reply on your behalf in three seconds, how would that benefit your lifestyle?"

Now of course if that's what they want and that's what they are looking for, they will pay attention to your words and syntax. However, and I must stress this, if you don't have any rapport with them, i.e. if you're "not getting on" with them, they won't care what you say because they are not paying attention to you. Furthermore, if there is no rapport, they will defend emotionally as they don't trust you yet and they'll probably make an excuse to leave!

If you have a solid rapport with them, however, they will be engaged with you. Sharing will build this, listening will seal it.

So, you can only ask closing questions when you have trust and rapport, and that's when you have to ask! And you will know when. How will you know? You will begin to feel it in your whole body, because you have practiced, role played, and actually gone out there and presented! You will get very good at sales when you immerse yourself in it and keep doing what works again and again!

When you have rapport, they will answer the question completely differently because they are engaged with you. They'll probably respond like this: "It would definitely help me, but tell me, how does it work? Can it really do what you just said?"

It will turn into a flowing conversation without any effort because the rapport is holding the engagement in place like glue.

The above response tells you that they are very interested, they trust you, and all you have to do now is prove that your offering can do what you just said it could.

We'll get to the proving part later as that is part of the process, as you must **satisfy logic** before you can fulfill or settle your customers' **confusion**.

Confusion is a state where the brain is in a flux between emotion and logic, desire and facts. Evidence will have to be presented in such a way that they can actually see the benefits working for them in their minds.

Yet the amazing and great thing with confusion is that it's a massive part of the buying process and a fantastic stage because it means they are about to learn something—and if you've engineered it properly, they are about to learn that your product can really help them!

They will start to see it in their mind and this will help them shift their consciousness. They will begin to have clearer **awareness** of what you've just shown them, and whenever they go through this process, they will become more sold on your product.

Stage 4: Confusion

Now I know this must sound really weird, what I've just told you above. Am I really saying that you have to confuse your clients?

Yes, I am!

Is this "normal"?

Yes, it is!

But it sounds a bit unconventional to me!

Yes it does, but convention does not sell products! Fantastic communication and understanding does!

This is the thing: yes, you've got to confuse, not with a mathematical equation—I don't mean that! I mean there'll be a **gap** in what you share with them and their understanding of it! In that gap, they'll have the opportunity to learn from you if you are there to clarify for them!

They are not going learn from you if you are not there for them. That's why I said before: you are a **resource** to them, not a manipulator, not a forceful salesperson. You are a resource that has to be trusted and used to help them solve their problem and improve their life. If you can really do that, you will have a customer for life as they will perceive you to be an expert in what you do! And people trust experts! You don't see car-owners taking their cars to be fixed by ten-year-old kids in the park, do you?

**Prospects want to know their problem can
be solved properly WITHOUT RISK!**

Your prospects will be confused throughout your presentation, because they are just learning what you've spent months getting your head around. They didn't attend your training course! You've got about 15 minutes to get their initial understanding of what you're doing. Yes, 15 minutes! If you can't get them to see how your offering could be good for them within that time, you can wave them bye-bye for life!

Isn't that ironic? I'll say it again: if you don't impress them and clarify for them, they will remain confused and buy from someone who can clear the picture for them, since they are buying for their needs. They definitely won't buy something if they can't see it fulfilling their needs or solving their problems. You will lose them, possibly and probably forever. And what's worse is that they'll tell everyone they know not to make the same mistake with you as they nearly did! Bad news has a way of traveling really fast!

I hope you are beginning to see where many salespeople are going wrong.

They don't understand the buying process.

And guess what? You're going to love this—every individual buys within his or her own cycle. That means that no two sales will be the same and the crucial variable to all this is cracking how to get rapport with your prospect.

Rapport creates the engagement, the focus, and the ease.

As soon as you get to build rapport and succeed, the buying process is similar with everyone. It's only the needs that vary and the way they see the benefits. What does that mean?

There are different **buying personalities**. Yes, there'll be people who are more logical and those who are more emotional, and you've got to figure out who you're presenting to before you present. If you're hitting a logical person with huge emotion triggers, they won't budge. Fortunately for you, I'm going to cover different buying personalities later in this book! But for now, just understand that you will have to adapt to your customers' buying process and buying personality.

All this may sound a little intense and complicated but I can tell you this: it's very easy to crack once you have immersed yourself in the knowledge you require in this book. It will become a part of you, like a kind of sixth sense, i.e. you will know what kind of person they are.

**You will "feel" it very quickly because you will spot
how they communicate—how they communicate is
how they would like to be communicated to!**

Let's say you have an older person who's talking very slowly. You will have to match that speed in your speech. Not exactly but thereabouts. The reason they are speaking slowly is not because they are retarded but because that's how they learn and clarify. Talking fast and loud in this engagement will kill you stone dead!

If you are confused now, that's fantastic as you are supposed to be. I've reached my objective then. Remember when you are confused, especially when you are immersed in learning something new, you will have far faster breakthroughs, you are about to learn very quickly, and that is what makes the difference to your bank account!

Now some of you may have heard this quote, but I'm using it because it is very powerful and something you must know before you can succeed.

Nearly 20 years ago, the author of the bestselling book, Future Shock, Alvin Toffler said, "The illiterate of the 21st century will not be those who cannot read and write, but those who cannot learn, unlearn and relearn."

Take heed in this, as your old, unsuccessful habits must be unlearned!

Stage 5: Awareness

In your presentation, there will be plenty of opportunity to present your benefits and features. There will also be plenty of opportunity for your prospect to ask questions. In the confusion state, it is very natural for the prospect to do so to really clarify what you are sharing with them. That's a sign that they are engaged. Let's go into a little psychology here.

If your prospect is not asking questions, one of three things is happening:

1. He is not interested at all
2. You've not achieved sufficient rapport, hence they are not engaged with you
3. They fully understand and are ready to buy!

Now, if you're not really getting any questions, it's time to stop what you're doing and ask them a **pattern breaker** question. This is to test how close they are or are not to buying.

What's a pattern breaker? It's a question that's designed to break or stop their existing thought pattern so you can discover what they are thinking. I must say at this stage I would normally use a strong closing question to really test the level of interest from my prospect.

For example, you could use;

"Can you see yourself using what I've just shown you today?"

"Would you prefer this way of doing it or another way?"

"In what way would this service help you?"

Or even stronger questions:

"If this fitted into your budget, am I looking at a new owner today?"

"What would stop you from buying this today?"

"What would this service have to look like for you to be able to purchase today?"

"Why are you not going to buy this today?"

There are a lot more questions in the second section and you really need this because you need a library of questions ready to be asked at any given moment.

How do you know what questions to ask and when?

That's a good question, and if you read, keep reading, and read this book again you will know when to ask and what to ask. You will know because you will have clues, and the clues will come from your prospect. Remember, only your prospect can tell you how and when to sell to them. Delivering a presentation without tuning into your prospect's needs is a complete waste of time.

Now let's get one thing straight here. This is not CSI (crime scene investigation). This is a science that can be learned easily once you are immersed in it. You'll be able to use all of your five senses very effectively to determine where your prospect is along the buying process and it is up to you to trust your senses.

You can only trust your senses when you have "trained" them what to detect, or what to be aware of.

Awareness is a two-way street!

What do I mean? Well, Your customers have to be completely aware of what they are about to buy before they can shift into a **sold** status and get their credit cards out. However, you must also be aware where they are in that buying process.

I've lost count of how many times I've seen salespeople just blab on and on because they are desperate to finish their presentation and get an answer, but end up completely shocked when the customer says no, that he's not interested! That is complete ignorance of the prospect's feelings and buying cycle and one of the most common mistakes you can make as a persuader!

There will be buying signals.

For the inexperienced among you, don't worry, I will explain this! For the experienced among you, just about to roll your eyes, you should read as well, as it's always good to go back to the basics! I repeat: **back to the basics**. You would be amazed how many average closers think going back to the basics is beneath them when it could be their greatest weapon!

The Buying Signal

A buying signal is something prospects "show" you when they are very interested in what you are offering or are ready to buy! Most times this will be disguised. For instance, a prospect is not going to come out and say to you, "If you can just answer this question for me and overcome my objection, I will definitely buy from you today and I will put the money on the table as I really want it!" Or, "I'm ready to buy now, please take my order!"

Remember, they are not going to say these things because they don't want to make a mistake in their purchase (and look foolish)! So all they are doing is clarifying what you are selling them. What they are really doing is focusing their mind to imagine a clear picture of themselves benefiting from the product. Their buying signals are a way for their brain to connect the dots and grasp what you are saying!

Now, if you don't get these buying signals and you don't know how to respond to them, you will not sell to them and you will wonder why. More interestingly, your prospects will wonder why they didn't buy it either!

This sounds silly, doesn't it? But the whole reason I wrote this book is to rant that it does matter how you sell to your prospects and communicate the need to know when to close them.

There's a famous saying in the selling world and you may have heard of it: "You have gone past the close". This means that you should have asked them to buy a while ago, or at least closed them on a benefit they really like.

You see, awareness is a two-way street. You have to be aware of your customers' buying cycle and you must do everything you can to get them on their buying cycle and make them aware of all your product's benefits.

If we go back a little in this book, I mentioned that ADD (attention deficit order) is rampant in the population because of the environment we live in— there are so many things vying for our attention. But there's a solution to this, of course.

When you have discovered a prospect's needs and hotspots, and are able to "illustrate" them in his mind so he can see them clearly, you will have his complete attention.

We'll talk more about buying signals later. They can come in many forms, but the three major ones are:

1. An objection
2. A question
3. A change in their body language

When you become aware of these three major signals, they will trigger your "when" radar to be very ready to close them imminently.

Stage 6: Sold!

Isn't that your favorite word in sales? A "sold" customer is someone who has just completed his order and paid in full because they understand your product, the benefits to them, and the presentation you have given. So the "sold" state comes when they are connected with you and your presentation. You are completely tuned in to their needs. They know you care about those needs, they trust you, and they are excited because their life will be improved. Nevertheless, the reason they are sold is because they have "seen" themselves benefiting directly from the product or service you are offering.

"Seeing" is what eludes most salespeople from becoming champion closers. They just don't "see" the customers' need to "see" for themselves, and so those salespeople will not learn how to communicate clearly to help their customer "see"!

Champions know WHEN to ask their customers to buy because they have seen their customers seeing the benefits in their mind!

In this book, you will learn that skill, you will apply it, and you will gain the experience necessary to change your results in a heartbeat. In practical terms, if you study this book for just one week, during the following week, your sales appointments will go better than you ever thought possible—and that's a guarantee!

SECTION II

THE ROAD-MAP TO CLOSING THE DEAL

CHAPTER 4

HOW DO YOU KNOW WHEN TO CLOSE THE DEAL?

"Recognize clearly your closing opportunities!"

H ere's a simple truth!

> **No desire means high resistance to closing. Plenty of desire means little or no resistance to closing!**

Desire starts from within you! Before you can even start thinking about closing any deals, three mandatory ingredients must exist.

1. Belief

You must have total faith in yourself and in your product. Remember, sales are a **transference of belief** from you to the customer. If you don't believe in what you are doing, then that is what you will transfer to them—a disbelief! How can they buy something you don't believe in?

2. Resource

Know your customer's needs (their Dominant Buying Motive) and fulfill them. That means you have to focus on your customer and allow them to see that you are there to fulfill their needs and help them achieve their goals. Pushing something they cannot see will never work, and they will see you as a pest they need to swat. DBM is Dominant Buying Motive OR the main reason the prospect will buy today from you. It is mentioned later, but I think a very brief explanation of it here is necessary to preview later chapters.

3. Rapport

You must have it before you can close. When you have rapport, you can say anything without fear of losing the deal. Without rapport, you will have a barrier to closing any deal. This barrier will not disappear if you don't know the code for unlocking it and creating great rapport between you and the client!

CLOSING SKILLS

RAPPORT BUILDING
& DESIRE BUILDING

Take a look at the diagram above and notice how effective closing works. It's actually really simple: you can't close without desire for the offering. You have to close **when they want it** and most certainly not before! So let's work on the "inner power" first, i.e. to create desire you must have the **belief** in yourself and that your product will really wow them and crucially **benefit** them!

Keep the diagram above handy so you can refer to it while you are reading. I'll be referring to it a lot during these next chapters.

CHAPTER 5

BELIEF

"Seeing is believing."

S o instead of being afraid of negative feedbacks from your customer like, "Marco, we need to think about this. We don't know whether it's for us or not"… instead of saying, "OK, Mr. Jones I understand, thanks for your time then"… instead of saying this very weak sentence (because this was what I used to say!), **I suddenly believed!** And this is what I said—please read on to find out what I said to close my first ever deal! (No, I'm not teasing.)

There are only two possible outcomes in any sales presentation:

1. You will sell to them and show them why, convincingly, they must own your product
2. They will sell to you and show you why, convincingly, they must not own your product

That means they will believe you or you will believe them!

Remember this: "The person with the most certainty in any engagement will always influence the other party!" And that certainty comes from your belief!

Whatever happens in your presentation, the result will be either number one or number two. Now I know what you would like it to be. I'm not going to ask a rhetorical question! What I can say in all confidence and experience is that it's all about psychology!

The bigger stone you throw into the pond, the bigger the ripples, the longer they will last, and the more they will wash over the smaller ripples!

Imagine those ripples are your thought-waves. The stronger thoughts you have, i.e. the more belief you have in what you are doing, the more the customer will begin to believe in you and your product. They will begin to see the benefits because they start to believe it!

In the customer's mindset: "Believing is seeing!"

Now look again at the diagram in Chapter 4. At the beginning of your presentation, your prospect's belief level is not there; they don't believe in what you are offering yet as they have not seen it inside their head. So it'll be alien to them as it doesn't belong in their system yet... until they've gone through a certain process with you.

You have to take them through a certain process in a certain way to inspire their belief system.

Before you even start presenting to anyone, your own belief level must be **ACTIVATED**. You have to believe that your products or service can really benefit the person you are talking to. You have to see your prospects using your products and benefiting from using them—and believe without any doubt that you are doing them a great service!

That's right, before your customer can see the benefits of your offer, you must see the benefits yourself first! How can you share anything with anyone if you can't see it and feel it?

For example, people can only really tell you of their experiences when they have experienced it. Recently, I celebrated New Year with my family and friends. And my other friends who weren't with me asked what I did to celebrate, i.e. where I went, what I did, and what it was like.

Now normally whatever I say to them, they will create a picture in their mind of what I was doing. So if I said to them, "Well, I went to a fantastic party at this lovely French restaurant called Bertrand's. The food was so nice it melted in my mouth! It was absolutely delicious! We had these beautifully cooked scallops in a savory sauce with some very fresh vegetables on the side. I don't normally eat carrots; however, they went so well with the scallops, I couldn't resist! You just had to be there, it was amazing!

"After dinner, the owner of the restaurant, Bertrand, decided to entertain us. Now you have to go to this restaurant just to see how wonderful and eccentric this guy is! He's bloody crazy, about five feet tall, balding, and very, very French—meaning, everything he said was coated with a fantastic French accent! He put on some old French songs and we all sang along in French! It was so funny to see our friends putting on a French accent!

"After dinner, Bertrand promised us the best fireworks display we had ever seen. And true to his French words, it was probably the most magnificent fireworks display we had ever seen, and it just kept going on and on. It wouldn't stop. It built to such an intensity I thought for a moment we were being attacked in an air-strike! It was just truly awesome!"

Now, what if I had just said, "I stayed in, watched TV and went to bed early"? Either way, they will picture whatever I said in their minds. They cannot help it!

Stop, rewind, analyze!
People think in pictures!

If you read back, when I started talking about a French restaurant, you probably pictured in your mind's eye your perception of what a typical French restaurant would look like: dark, luxurious, plenty of atmosphere, small, cozy, and violin or accordion music in the background, or something like that. All I said was "French restaurant". Your mind will not see the words "French restaurant". But it will see a picture, a reference to what a French restaurant looks like... so that you can relate to me and share my experience!

When I started talking about the food, I didn't go into a lot of detail here. But what I did mention was probably enough for you to picture those scallops and get your taste buds going. A picture in your mind might have been the scallops on the plate in the hot, steaming sauce, and you taking the fork and putting some in your mouth, and then chewing the food slowly, tasting so good that you tilted your head back and savored the taste and made some sort of sound of pleasure like, "Mmmmhh... yum."

We automatically think in pictures, and in those pictures you will also sense other experiences such as taste, smell, and touch!

A champion, top-performing salesperson absolutely knows they must be able to describe the benefits to the prospect at a level where the prospect can relate and see the benefits themselves. The best route to doing this is when you have total belief in yourself and what you are doing!

So how do you get that kind of belief? Well, before I start talking about that, you must understand the "belief requirements".

The first belief requirement: You must believe in yourself!
The second belief requirement: You must believe in what you are selling!

Let's make this very, very clear:

- If you don't believe in yourself or your product, your bank balance will have exactly the amount you deserve—not a lot!
- If you don't believe in yourself but you believe in your product, your bank balance will have exactly the amount you deserve—not a lot either!

- If you believe in yourself but you don't believe in your product, your bank balance will have exactly the amount you deserve—again, not a lot!
- If you believe in yourself and your product, your bank balance will have exactly the amount you deserve—a whopping lot more!

So the only question here is, because this is what it comes down to: Do you want to have a freaking whole lot more money in your bank account or not? Sorry to be so direct... well, actually I'm not really sorry for that because you need to hear (or read) this and stamp it into your brain until you cannot think about anything else!

To have lots of money in your bank account is like this: every time you go to the ATM, you are smiling and saying, "Yes!" with a punch in the air, so much so, that the people queuing behind you would think that you had won the lottery. Then you have to start believing, you have to have the faith, and please note: to write about the ATM feeling above, I had to experience that myself, get the picture in my mind, and then describe it to you!

Trust me, it is a phenomenal feeling, and I will never forget what a great friend of mine told me. His name is Mano. He was one of the first guys I hired in a new project I started in Malaysia some years back.

He said to me, "Marco, I will never forget walking to the ATM, putting in my card, and seeing my account balance, three months after I started with you. I thought I had mistakenly typed in the wrong account number and was seeing somebody else's account. I looked at the figure in disbelief, I was so confused. I just stood there for about five minutes scratching my head, wondering where the hell the money came from! And then it hit me that I had made and earned that money working with you! It was the best feeling I have ever had in my life! I had never made that kind of money before, it was like a miracle! Thank you for helping me get there!"

Mano told me this story some years after I first met him. It made me feel brilliant, really great, because that made me realize that I had given Mano a great gift: I had transferred my belief to him! But I could only do this because I had great belief in myself and what I was selling.

So, how do you believe in yourself?

Well, do you believe you can raise your hand to your head? If you think you can raise your hand to your head, you will do it easily, effortlessly, without even thinking about it, because it is already "programmed" just like we talked about in the beginning of this book! Now, if you have any doubt that you can raise your hand, you won't do it, you will hesitate. You may lift it a little, but then not follow through because you have more disbelief than belief.

Believe it or not, because of some health issues or disabilities, there are some people who cannot raise their hand to their head no matter what they do. However, there are some with the same disabilities who have raised their hands to their heads.

So why are these people different? Because
they believed! They suddenly believed they could!

Gabriel Gargam is one such person. He suddenly believed he could change—although his disability was far worse. He was paralyzed from the waist downwards, his spine severely injured. He had visited all the doctors he could and none of them could give him any hope. The doctors "knew" there was no medical, scientific cure available for someone with his condition.

Most people at this stage would resign themselves never to walk again. The experts in his environment said no. His friends didn't believe. No one believed he could get better… except his mother! She asked him to go to Lourdes. You know, the place in France where so-called miracles happen.

Gabriel refused because he had lost hope. He was in despair and had lost heart. But his mother insisted and looked him in the eye with a faith Gabriel was not used to.

So he went to Lourdes. Within 30 minutes he struggled and raised himself to his feet. And within 24 hours, he was walking normally!

Now before you go laughing and say this is ridiculous, I can share with you thousands of other similar miracles which have happened and are completely true!

Gabriel was examined by over 60 doctors. This cure could not be explained scientifically. It just happened… because Gabriel suddenly believed. He suddenly believed the power was within him and it was entirely in his hands whether he walked again or not!

It is the belief within you that brings outwards material results. Now I can give you the sexiest and cleverest tactic you have ever seen, but nothing—I repeat nothing—will replace the power of belief!

If you've learned new skills and are practicing them, but you don't have any faith, or you keep saying, "I can't do this. It's not right. It's not me. It's just too difficult," then you just don't have any belief at all. You have given up before having even started!

Because it's easy when you believe and you know how.

You may be wondering why I'm spending so much time on this and going on and on about something you think you know.

I am doing this because I was doing what I thought was right and struggling to pay my bills. It was so bad that at one point early in my sales career, I had no money to pay the train fare to go home or eat any more than a tin of peas. The lowest point in my life was when I had to open a tin of peas and put them between two slices of white stale bread for my dinner. It was the only thing I had to eat all day and I was starving.

I was a victim and I wouldn't go to anybody for help because I didn't think they wanted to hear my sad story. But my life changed. I mean, my life radically turned 360 degrees in the space of 24 hours because someone at my workplace saw something in me. He saw some potential in me and knew deep down he could help me at that precise time, and he knew it was the perfect time to help. He knew when I needed the help. He closed me at the right time, because he knew I was so "hungry" to improve!

He took me aside, gave me a book, and said, "Read this book, but tell no one. Read it from cover to cover as fast as you can. Don't stop reading it; keep reading it. And when you've finished reading it, read it again and then see how you feel."

It was a strange experience. Yes, I did wonder—why must I tell no one? However, **he got my attention! Big time.** He got my curiosity and he was the top-performing salesperson in my company, so I felt very humbled when he approached me, the worst-performing salesperson in the company! He must know something, I thought.

At that point, I **had nothing to lose!**

And it was at this point, at the point where I had nothing to lose, where my life changed instantly—literally overnight. I read the book. I locked myself in a room, told no one, and read the book. As I read the words, the greatest lesson I've ever learned was spelled out to me, and I had the most profound realization. I **suddenly believed**, and I knew I had the power to change my own life. I became excited—very excited—and for the first time since I had started the job, I was actually looking forward to seeing my next prospect! I couldn't wait to share my belief with them!

Normally I was afraid and filled with dread at having to meet any new prospect and present to them, but this time I just knew I had nothing to lose, and for the first time, I had absolutely **no fear** whatsoever. I actually was not afraid of any resistance the prospect might give me. I was not afraid of any objections at all because I believed in myself. I was complete. I didn't need the prospect's confirmation that I was a nice guy. For the first time, I was not there to be a nice guy... I was there to help my prospects improve the quality of their life and I believed that with total conviction! I mean, there was no doubt I was going to be a resource to my customers; I was going to help them live a better life—and I did!

Read this next paragraph very, very carefully!
It's triply, quadruply important!

So instead of being afraid if I had a negative response from my customer, for example, if they were to tell me, "Marco, we need to think about this. We don't know whether it's for us or not," and then I would say, "Ok, Mr. Jones, I understand, thanks for your time then." But instead of saying this very weak sentence (because this was what I was saying before!), I **suddenly believed!**

I said, "Thank you so much for being honest with me, Mr. Jones. You know what? Everyone who comes to see me and takes my presentation says exactly the same thing as you, at the same time. And normally I would say to them, 'Ok, thanks for your time.' But do you know what? I'm not going to say that today. Do you know why, Mr. Jones?"

Mr. Jones's response: "Errmmm, no, why?"

"Because I suddenly believe in what I am doing. I believe in this company and I believe what I'm showing you today will completely change your life for the better because I've seen my colleagues' customers benefit so much, and quite honestly, all our other customers say exactly the same as you when they come in, and they end up being our best customers and recommend **all their contacts** to come here and see how good it is for themselves!"

Now, technically, this might have been the wrong thing to say or the wrong words in the wrong order, but—and this is a big but—the way I said those words was electrifying! I mean, when I was saying them, goose-bumps appeared all over my body! I felt the most awake I had ever felt, and I was feeling very emotional. In fact, tears were welling up in my eyes. I was feeling so good about myself for the first time in years, and I didn't care if they got out of their chairs and walked away—it didn't matter! And it didn't matter for the first time in years because I knew the next one would buy!

In actuality, they didn't walk away; they actually sat there, completely stunned for a few seconds, but it seemed like minutes!

After their shock, they said, "Ok, Marco, errmmm, tell us why those other people are so happy, tell us more, how does it work?"

Now I was shocked! I was shocked because it was the very first time anyone had shown any interest in what I was showing them. It was the first time I had a question! And when this question came, my belief got stronger and my goose-bumps were like golf-balls! It was a very powerful moment for me and my life has never been the same since. It changed entirely. I then proceeded to sell my prospects. They bought the biggest package we had, and then the next ones bought and the next! Within six months, yes, just six months, I was presented with the "salesperson of the year" award at our annual conference!

True faith always shows up when challenged!

I won this award for three years running. I became the youngest sales manager in the company at the age of 23. All the others were in their 40s. And within three years, I was one of the top leaders in the company.

Yes, you've probably heard or read this kind of story before. The victim suffering and then taking that heroic journey, that yellow brick road to enlightenment, but what's wrong with that? Let me tell you, that is life and that is why life is so addictive, because you have the power to determine any kind of life you want, at any time! And that was my greatest discovery!

A lot of people never realize this and die young without ever finding happiness and success. Too many people in this world end up being a slave living other people's lives.

I implore you not to do that and to start taking responsibility for your own actions. **No one else** will do it for you. It is down to you. There is no other way. There is no other easy way. This is the easiest path, and it can happen at **lightning speed** if you know you have nothing to lose! And the fact is, you don't, because if you don't use this book, if you don't read it again, you're going to keep getting the same results again and again. Why? Because you will still be in the same pattern and the same program. It is inevitable that you will end up in the same place, time and again!

If you use one idea from this book and it doesn't put more money into your bank account, what would you have lost? Well, the cost of this book. But don't worry about that... because I'm going give you a guarantee. Yes, if it doesn't improve your sales within 15 days, I'm going to return all your money! So what have you got to lose? That, my friend, is when you will start to improve! And if your bank account increases only 10 percent a month by reading this book, would it be worth it? What would that extra 10 percent give you?

When I learned the power of belief, my income increased 1,000 percent in a week. It couldn't have gone any lower. Well, okay, I'm telling a lie: I was getting 100 pounds per week for four weeks, then commission only. I had already received my last check, so it could have been zero the following week, but it went from 100 to 1,000 pounds in five days, and it kept increasing!

> **The only traitor you'll have in your life and in your sales process is yourself if you start doubting your ability.**

As soon as you doubt anything you are doing, stop doing it! Because you won't succeed at all!

Start selling only when you BELIEVE in what you are doing!

So, how do you believe in your product or service?

An interesting question, isn't it? You already know that if you don't believe in your product, your bank balance will be seriously affected, so why would you want to sell something you don't believe in, right?

If you are in a job which you don't believe in, don't have faith in the company, and feel that your product isn't benefiting the customer in any way, you must be getting paid a lot of money! Either that or you are horribly afraid of losing this job and are not able to get another one.

Let me tell you something very clearly:

> **No amount of money will make you believe in something if you can't see it!**

If you are getting paid a lot of money for what you are doing, and you don't believe in what you are doing, **you'll get found out.**

If you are afraid of losing your job because it pays the bills but you hate what you are doing and you don't believe in it, **you'll get found out.**

What do I mean that you'll get found out?

Simply this: It's extremely challenging to keep doing something you don't believe in. It's "soul destroying". It's very bad for your health because your heart does not want to do it, yet your brain is forcing your heart to do it even though you know it's **completely wrong!**

Do you know what the biggest killer is on the planet today? If you don't know it already, let me tell you: it is heart disease. It's the biggest killer, even bigger than cancer!

Heart Dis-Ease

Or a heart that's troubled, that will never feel **love** or **passion** because it is doing something it doesn't believe in!

Do you know what causes heart disease? Stress. Do you know what stress is? It is the ultimate conflict between heart and brain, between conscious and subconscious, between logic and emotion!

Remember, emotion is the driving force that makes you take a certain action. If it feels right, you will do it. **Your logic will just calculate if it fits with your mindset**. Then your intellect will tell you, "Yes that is great. This is what you need to do logically to get there!" This happens inside you whether it is to learn more about something, change your behavior slightly, go a certain way, etc.

Let me give you an example from the earlier chapters. How many times have you heard or seen a successful accountant completely give up what he's doing and decide to do something completely different, so different that it shocks his friends and family? Let me tell you, this happens all the time!

How many people do you see in the world who are not happy with what they are doing, and they are just doing it to survive, to pay the bills, because of fear?

Far too many people in this world allow FEAR to drive their next choice—the fear of no money, no job, no respect, and no life.

The human potential is to live to 130 years old. Yes, you heard correctly. It is possible to live to 130 years healthily, with all your faculties intact! So why is it that most of the population live to only around 75 years old?

If stress is the cause of heart disease, which is the biggest killer, then it must be because emotionally and spiritually, we are killing ourselves! It's been medically and chemically proven that if we experience stress, our bodies release adrenalin (the "fight or flight" hormone) and cortisol (the "keep awake at all costs" hormone). These two hormones are nature's ingenious way of protecting our life if we are in grave danger. So if we have an accident and are bleeding heavily, cortisol is released to help us get help! Adrenaline is released to make us run away from danger or fight it.

So why are these hormones released into our bodies on a daily basis?

If you don't know the answer to this, please allow me to spell it out for you: The reason you have these hormones in large quantities in your bodies every day is to help you survive a slow death of continued conflict! More simply put:

You are doing something you don't want to do and this is killing you!

You see, by doing something you don't believe in, your heart will not help you do it, because it knows it is not right for you. You body will release those survival hormones to help you stop doing it as soon as possible!

The people carrying the most pain in this world are not the people with cancer or disabilities. They are the people who have lost their passion, the people who are just trying to survive! If you don't believe me, here are the latest global statistics.

Out of every 100 people at the end of a 40-year working period:

- 1 is financially independent (i.e. will never have any money worries)
- 4 are still working (but not because they want to)
- 36 are dead
- 59 are "dead broke" (i.e. living off on credit cards, loans, handouts, welfare, etc.)

I'm banging my fists on the table like a gorilla right now! Why? Because I have to get this through to you and everyone else:

When you BELIEVE in yourself, in what you are doing and SELLING, you WILL BECOME RICH and FINANCIALLY FREE!

Why am I saying this? Why I am so passionate about this? Because sales is one of the only professions where your income is unlimited and determined by your passion and belief. It is unlimited because eventually there can be many people selling for you in your team, and you will create **residual income**—more income than you ever thought possible, just because you suddenly believe!

Never ever feel that sales is bad or that sales is not a worthy profession. Sales is the oldest and most common profession on this planet because people have to persuade and influence others all the time in every situation. Sales are what keeps an economy alive. Sales are what pays for your fancy office and your salary. Let's see what else involves selling.

- Teachers "selling" their knowledge to students to make them smarter.
- Engineers "selling" their skills and knowledge to their companies and clients.
- Employees "selling" themselves to their bosses to earn promotions.
- Parents "selling" to their children to stay away from cigarettes.
- Advertisers "selling" ad spots.
- CEOs "selling" their ideas to their boards of directors.
- Guys "selling" themselves to girls to get dates.
- A business partner "selling" an idea to his colleagues.
- Doctors "selling" their treatments.
- A lawyer "selling" his previous results and how he can do the same for you.
- A computer serviceman "selling" you his repair skills.
- A financial planner "selling" his investment package as better than the rest.
- A network marketer "selling" to sponsor you.
- A religious leader "selling" the reasons why you should convert to his religion.
- An individual "selling" his worth to a bank to obtain a loan.
- A child "selling" to her parents why she deserves a nice present.

Sales are simply a transference of belief.

Anyway, sorry for ranting, but I feel it is important to really spell out how critical your belief system is to close more business. Most books don't really get this by the scruff of the neck, by drilling in what the first steps should be to become a champion closer. Champion closers will all tell you categorically that **belief** is everything. It is the oil in the engine. Without oil, the car will seize up! Belief will get you going and make everything work for you. It will lubricate your journey like "grease lightning"!

Now where was I? Ah yes, how do you believe in your product? I think that deserves another small chapter!

CHAPTER 6

BELIEVING IN YOUR PRODUCT!

"BE A RAVING FAN of what you are selling!"

Following my belief in belief, believing in your product is an extension of your own faith in yourself. Your customer will not buy your product without it being presented by a qualified salesperson.

A **qualified salesperson**? Yes, as well as the customer being qualified, you have to be qualified as well.

Now here's a huge misconception held by millions of organizations around the world: Companies think a professional, qualified salesperson is somebody who knows the product inside out—all their features, pricing, and benefits— and is able to present all this knowledge to the prospect without making a single mistake!

**What they—and most salespeople—don't realize
is that is actually the least important factor!**

Yes, you have to know what you are talking about, but how many times have you been bored senseless listening to a "qualified salesperson" explain how a product works to you? Prospects don't want to know how these things work— they just want to know how **it'll benefit them**! For example, if you are looking at a mobile phone, you don't want or need to know how it's able to receive a picture or another person's voice from across the world. Heck, I don't know, and I don't care to know!

What people want to know is how it can benefit them! Is it easy and convenient to use? Will it save them time, and is it affordable?

**Prospects will only know if it can benefit them
if you can see the benefits yourself first!**

You have got to see the benefits first! That means you have seen it work yourself, and when your belief system is totally satisfied, then it can do the job! I hope you understand that it is far easier to sell something when you are a "raving fan" yourself!

Enthusiasm is a result of belief!

I know this sounds really basic, but I'll say it again: the basics are what make the difference between a genuine smile at the ATM machine or the fear of approaching a machine which may eat your card!

To become an enthusiastic, raving fan of your product, you will have to "see" for yourself first by using your product before you can transfer that belief to your prospect.

**You can't transfer money from your bank account
to another if you don't have anything there!**

This sounds ridiculous, doesn't it? However, you would be stunned at how many so-called "salespeople" have a complete lack of enthusiasm for what they are doing because their heart is not in it.

I can't forget early in my sales career when I asked one of my first customers why he purchased from me. He said, "The product is great, Marco, but really it wasn't about that. It was about the belief I saw in you. I could see in your eyes you were sold on it, and you believed in what you were doing so much that you were willing to spend a long time with me showing me your belief was true! I could just see it in your eyes and I knew then I should buy it!"

Do you see what I mean? You have to "see" it first before they can. Now, let me touch a little here on **enthusiasm**!

You cannot get enthusiastic about something if you are not excited by it and emotionally attached to it. You cannot ignite passion without the light of belief and feeling.

Enthusiasm counts for over 50 percent of your sale!

Yes, it's true! So if you work out the math, you actually don't need product knowledge to get a "yes" from your customer—you just need to find the **belief** in it! When you have belief in the company and the products you are representing, your prospect will be far more comfortable buying as they know their money is safe.

You can only close a sale effectively when you have belief.

It's also interesting to note the last four letters of the word enthusiasm are I-A-S-M, which really means: "I Am Sold Myself!"

So get yourself sold! To do that, here's a few rules of thumb. You should **always, always** research before starting to sell any product. Unfortunately, most salespeople don't bother doing this!

1. The Company Track Record

Get on "Google" and search for the company that manufactures your product or service and get as much information as you can. Print all the materials you can from the internet and look through them. Now if something is good, people are going to share it with others; they are going to write about it! However, if something is bad they will generally write a lot more about it and why it is bad! Find out how people and companies (if you are in corporate sales) rate the product.

Most of all, get to the nitty-gritty of the company, e.g. who are the directors and owners? What is their background and experience? What success has the company enjoyed? Very importantly, how healthy is their balance sheet? If you don't know what a balance sheet is, let me quickly explain.

It is how much cash versus how much debt the company has. If the company's debts exceed its assets, you have a problem. If the company has assets but no cashflow, you have a problem. A healthy balance sheet means the company has plenty of cash reserves and good assets, i.e. they own properties and other good companies. Then they are here to stay! A company that is healthy will have all records up to date and their paid-up capital will be good!

Go for an **award-winning company** that sells **award-winning products**! Good companies will normally have achieved a certain status in the community and many will have won decent awards for either their innovation or quality.

Go to their office! Make a trip to preferably their headquarters. Check their office out. See how it's arranged. Is everything clean, professional, and smart? How many offices have you been to that are not like this? There are many!

2. Test Their Customer Service

You know, I'm still amazed that people do not look at this as an indicator to tell you how great a company is! Look at it like this. You have just sold a product to a qualified prospect. Then they call your company because they have a problem or a question. They call, and are put through to an operating system which has a menu saying something like this: "For inquiries press 1; for service press 2; for payments press 3; for feedback press 4 (this is a posh word for complaints!); for other services press 5...." They have absolutely no chance to talk to a **human being**! Some just give up trying after being put on hold forever, or get transferred to the umpteenth "right person"!

Has that happened to you? I would bet on it! I have lost count of how many times this has happened to me—and I'm talking about so-called "big" companies!

It's really simple. Big and established companies who have controlled the market will profit take (take as much money as you can and do not spend it on your customer service, buy fast cars and stuff, etc.) and won't focus so much on their customer service. They will sit back and get comfortable. In this world? Yes, it happens!

Usually companies that want to grow have an "aggressive" focus on customer service, because they know that's how to win the market and the community.

I'm not going to mention a particular company here, but most big mobile phone telcos have some of the worst service I have ever seen and experienced! Their customer service is rubbish, yet they make 55 percent profit. I know this because I've done my research, and on prepaid service, they make 65 percent from you! You see, they know you will need to talk, so they don't spend money on the service you deserve as a customer.

I don't want to go into details here, so let me keep it simple. If you cannot get through to the company via their phone or email, you are going to have big problems keeping your customers. How can you believe in such a company?

The simple answer is: you can't! There's no way you are going to be confident in selling their product if you cannot speak to their "front line".

Front line? The first point of contact with any company after their salespeople is their customer service staff. How the customer service staff handles you over the phone is an exact guide of how their management works.

One of the major reasons I have been so successful in my field is because the companies which I've turned around did not focus on their human resources, did not care about them, and did not value them. They valued money and saving money above all else.

Here is a funny but true story. A few years ago, on a contract project which I was working on, the upper management of that company, including the board of directors, sent a memo around to all their staff, asking them to think of "10 ways the company could save money".

What kind of a message is this? Well, as you can imagine, a "sinking ship" message! Let's throw the rubbish off the side so we can sink more slowly!

So I met with the board and the upper management and said to them, "Think of 10 ways the company can make money!"

They all looked at me completely stunned and couldn't answer. Now that is a sad state of affairs by any stretch of the imagination. If they had sent that memo out first, it would have gotten a completely different reaction from their staff, because it was a more positive message! Their people would have felt inspired and looked at the future and growth and opportunities—instead of curling up in the corner recycling photocopy paper!

3. Test Their Website & Social Media.

Believe it or not, there are companies out there that are still without a website! Has your jaw lifted up from the floor yet? Surprising, but it's not unusual!

There are many more companies out there that display on their webpage, "website under construction"! This is basically telling you they can't be bothered or haven't got around to it yet. Now that is not a forward-thinking company or one you should be involved in!

There are even more companies out there that have not touched their websites literally for years! You can normally tell this because they have no updates, no newsletters, no blogs, or more "interesting" news, very few followers on their Facebook and Instagram accounts and hardly relevant content, they have an old address or contact numbers on their homepage! "That's terrible," I hear you say? Very common indeed!

Moving on from this, there are also many companies out there where their websites are "under maintenance". Let me tell you the truth here: websites do need maintaining; however, if they are down for more than a day, you will have serious problems with this company. You see, any company can take a website down, but a decent company has a backup website, while the old one is being renewed or upgraded.

So there you have it. A company's website and its social media channels should reflect it in a good light, should show visuals and features of their products, their track record, promotions, and should be up to date! Millions of salespeople fail to do this simple research and end up a victim of the wrong company!

The company is a reflection of you! You are a reflection of the company!

Prospects and customers will associate a good company with you and look upon you with respect. They will also associate a bad company with you or any problem they have had with one of "your" products and look at you with skepticism!

Perception is everything to your prospect!

4. Test Their Products

It might be the case that you already are using one of their products. However, if you are not, don't accept from the person who's hiring you that his company's products are the best! If you don't try and sample any of the products or services, you will be at a great disadvantage! Because you cannot "see" how the customers will benefit!

Whatever it is you are selling, please, please, make sure you use it first. Make sure you have a complete demonstration first before you start selling anything! Of course, if your company makes ceilings, you can't test those out, can you? Nevertheless, you can visit their existing customers and ask if they are happy with their ceilings!

It's just simple common sense. It's something you will never regret doing. Plus, if the company and their products are really good, it'll increase your level of belief and make your job easy, because now you have faith in what you are doing, in what you are selling, and in who you are working with! Can you now see how this will help you so much in knowing when to close the sale? (That was a trial close question, by the way, something which we're going to learn later in this book.)

Knowing when to close is also knowing beyond any doubt that your products will deliver and normally exceed what your prospect is looking for! When you have that kind of **unshakable belief**, your customers will find it very challenging to say no. When you become so good at transferring that unswerving passion for what you believe in, your customers will start to see they were very fortunate to have met you! They will also start to "see" that you can become a huge resource for them now and in the future—and that is another reason they will want to do business with you!

5. Their Compensation (Your paycheck!)

This is important. Don't put down the book for a rest until you have read this!

It might have hit you already that money is quite important! Some people think money is not as important as many other things. However, coming from a background of bankruptcy—yes, I have been bankrupt—I can share with you that money is phenomenally fantastic when you have it!

Why? If you don't know the reason yet, let me spell it out for you:

Money lubricates your chosen lifestyle!

So if you want to take off and visit the Hanging Gardens of Babylon, the Great Pyramids of Giza, or a nice mini-break, you'll probably realize there is nothing worse than having a limited "budget" when you go on holiday. It's not nice to always hang out at the cheapest joints and go to a supermarket on vacation! Similarly, it's also extremely unpleasant to receive several phone calls and letters telling you that if you don't pay soon, your credit cards will be barred. Or worse, being put on the blacklist where you can't get credit to buy a house or whatever else you desire!

How a company pays you is a very interesting subject indeed, because sales is a vocation that depends on you getting results. So, if you are not paid on getting results, you are just being paid a basic salary. Then, may I ask you, why are you doing it?

You are what you are paid!

CHAPTER 7

YOU ARE WHAT YOU ARE PAID!

"And this will increase your belief system"

There was an experiment done recently in the UK by a large carmaker called Daewoo. Their advertising stated clearly that they don't give discounts, they don't pay their salespeople commission, and what you see is what you get—true value!

Literally millions were spent on this sales strategy! Can you guess how successful the campaign went?

It was the biggest flop imaginable! Customers stayed away, and even when they did go, they found the salespeople not eager to service them or even show them the car! Even worse, when customers asked if there was any discount, the salespeople said, "No, sorry there is no discount!"

Let's look at this more closely.

1. Discounts

I don't know about you, but when I'm buying a big-ticket item, like a car or a house, I like to get a **good deal**! That means I love to haggle and be able to negotiate something better than the original price. You know what, sometimes it doesn't have to be a cash discount!

I remember when I bought a lovely BMW some years back there was a fantastic BMW baby seat in the car showroom. Thinking of my newborn baby, I said to the sales guy—as he was being difficult, "Hey, if you throw in that baby seat I'll have the car today!"

You guessed it. I got the car and the great baby seat—and a happy wife!

Basically, I had fulfilled my need!

The thing is that the customer feels far better when he feels that he has got a really good deal. In any purchase, the customer needs to feel that he won something from you. This really clinches the deal, and I don't believe I have ever in the last 20 years seen it any different! (We'll talk more about this later under closing needs).

So when the customers went to Daewoo and they got nothing—not even some enthusiasm from the salespeople—they felt lost. There was no fun! Worse still, they didn't get what they went for… a good car!

2. Commissions

A salesperson without a commission package is like a Ferrari without an engine! Both simply do not work!

Can you imagine working your little tush off closing a sale that has taken you hours, days, weeks or even months to close—and not getting a commission? How would you feel if that happened to you? Where is the reward, the recognition?

Salespeople are a breed apart. They need attention, they need connection, and most of all, they need recognition! And part of that recognition, besides a decent pat on the back from the boss, is a bucket full of cash!

I can't apologize for sounding like this, because being rewarded properly for one's efforts really does inspire a salesperson to get better, love the product more, and be more loyal to the company—and **get better results**!

A lot of salespeople have the misconception that if a company pays commission only, without a basic salary, then it is not a very good company.

How wrong this is! And what an opportunity those salespeople are missing out on because some of the biggest and best companies in the world pay their sales team commission only. But they pay big commissions frequently and on time!

In one of his recent newsletters, Brian Tracy talked about his son who had just left school and was going for his first job. (By the way, you should subscribe to his newsletters. He's really good. You'll learn a lot. I love the guy.). Anyway, Brian's son asked him what he should do. Without any hesitation whatsoever, Brian advised him to start door-to-door commission-only sales for a great company he knew well and had done some work for.

His son took his advice, and got tons and tons of rejections. His father supported him and eventually his son started closing sales and was suddenly growing rich. Within weeks, he had his own sales team and was making in excess of $1,000 a week.

Why did Brian do this? Because he knew, like me, "commission only" is the fastest way to learn **how to sell and get results**, be more confident, and be altogether a far more resourceful, happy, and better person!

His son thanked him a lot, especially when at only 18 years old, his friends were struggling to pay their bills and still relying on their parents!

You see, the best way to learn is to do the thing you don't know and learn from your mistakes.

"Commission only" is a **fantastic way** to learn fast and make lots more money, especially if you have the right support system. A good support system is important because many people give up just as they are about to have a huge breakthrough!

I have never had a salary. I have always worked on commission only. Oh, wait a minute, yes, there was one time when I was consulting for a huge company and they paid me a salary, but I made sure the commissions were far higher. In fact, the commissions made up 90 percent of my income!

Stay away from companies that limit your income, that offer a great basic and commission. Usually their commission is not so great and you can only afford the bills you have each month!

Make this your mantra:

GREAT SALESPEOPLE DON'T WORK FOR GREAT BASIC SALARIES! THEY WORK FOR GREAT COMMISSIONS THAT ARE PAID OFTEN AND ON TIME! SUCCESSFUL SALESPEOPLE THRIVE ON INCENTIVES!

Reminder! You can only close the deal effectively when:

- YOU HAVE THE RIGHT ATTITUDE
- YOU HAVE MASTERED THE LEARNING PROCESS
- YOU RECOGNIZE THE CUSTOMER'S BUYING PROCESS
- YOU FOLLOW THE ROADMAP
- YOU HAVE COMPLETE BELIEF IN YOURSELF
- YOU HAVE COMPLETE BELIEF IN YOUR PRODUCT
- YOU HAVE AN AWESOME COMMISSION PACKAGE

CHAPTER 8

RESOURCE

"... totally and without interruption!"

Have you ever met and talked to people who weren't really talking to you? You know what I mean. They know you are there, they can see you, but you seem to be the least important "thing" to them in the world. They know you are talking, but don't seem to know when it's their turn to talk. They kind of talk over you all about themselves, and by the end of the encounter, they don't know your name, don't acknowledge you again, and you are left standing there, completely embarrassed by it all.

Don't you just hate that? Don't you just want to disappear when that happens? Don't you feel like you have done something wrong? Don't you feel insulted sometimes and just want to run back up to that person and say, "Hey, who the hell do you think you are? That was bloody rude!"?

How would you feel if that happened to you all the time? Would you feel good about yourself or crappy?

The answer is really obvious, isn't it?

When people treat you like that, it actually lowers your self-esteem, and it makes you look inwards to see if there's anything wrong with you!

Now here's another interesting question. If you met someone like that, would you really want to spend any length of time with that person? Would you want to share your secrets and share your dreams? Or would you close yourself off?

So, if you met a salesperson like that, who didn't acknowledge you, how would you feel?

Essentially, would you buy?

A very close friend of mine, some years back, had a similar experience. She was looking for a new car and knew exactly what she wanted: a silver four-door Alfa Romeo. It was etched in her brain and she could "see" it really clearly—she knew what she wanted!

After driving for over an hour, she found a showroom that had the exact model which she was looking for. So she went in to talk about price. And guess what she found when she went in?

Not a single salesperson approached her! Not one of them showed any enthusiasm or interest in speaking to her. And no, they weren't selling Daewoos!

In the end, my friend had to approach their office and ask about the car! Still the sales staff seemed uninterested. She asked how much the car was. And have a guess what the salesperson said. You won't believe it!

He said, almost immediately, "Is your husband not with you?"

My friend was totally taken aback; she didn't know what to say! She was completely aghast—hypnopompic! (Remember this word? It's the state you are in just before you wake up.).

Eventually, as she gathered her thoughts and controlled her anger, she let him have it. "What does it matter if my husband is with me or not, I make my own decisions! And now, I'm making the decision that I'm never going to buy a car from you! Good day!"

You probably can gather by now that my friend isn't the "stay-at-home, make-dinner" kind of woman. She's someone who values her independence.

That salesperson's question killed dead the sale he would have had IF he paid her attention.

My friend was so incensed that she sped off to the next showroom. They didn't have the car she wanted originally. It was close but a different color, and $5,000 more expensive! But she bought that car!

Why did she buy? She told me she bought because the salesperson understood her needs and helped (by the fact that she was another woman), because the first thing my friend did when she got into that showroom was tell a complete stranger all about her bad experience at the previous place!

Now, this salesperson was very smart because she didn't assume anything. She didn't assume that my friend would buy the car or not. She didn't assume a "husband" was necessary. And she certainly didn't assume that my friend was crazy and needed psychological help!

What she did do, however, was show the utmost attention to my friend by focusing on her completely. She looked at her mouth as it uttered every syllable and she listened, not just casually listened; she really, really listened and showed that she really cared for my friend and her predicament. My friend later told me, "She really understood me. She really made me feel fantastic. She got me out of that bad place and she wouldn't talk until I had finished what I was saying. Even when I interrupted her when she was speaking, she stopped to listen to me. And that made my decision for me. I really wanted to buy a car from this person because I knew she would look after me, I knew she was genuine! And what was really refreshing is, she even told me she didn't have the car I wanted, or the color and she couldn't get it—she was bloody honest!

"Once I knew she respected me and wasn't going to rip me off, I asked to show me something else similar and she did. It was more expensive and it wasn't the color. But I liked her, and I actually started to prefer this car which she was showing me. So I bought it!

"The only thing going through my mind as soon as I bought my new car was driving it to the previous showroom and telling the silly sales guy, 'BIG MISTAKE!' just like out of that movie **Pretty Woman**!"

I was laughing when she told me that she did exactly that. I would have paid handsomely to see the look on his face when she did it! But that really made her day complete!

You may read my friend's story above and think, "Nah, that's not true!" Well, I'm telling you it is very true and I'm also telling you this **happens a lot**! Your competition will benefit a lot if you don't know when to focus on the customer!

So how do you focus on your prospective customer?

1. Value Every Opportunity To Meet Someone New!

This has to come first and these are where the first mistakes are made. A stranger is a friend and customer in disguise. You must value any new meeting you may have with any new person you meet or are introduced to.

Friends buy, strangers don't.

What I'm saying is a new person can add income to your bank account and will know lots of other people who can also add income to your bank account! So don't be so casual when you meet someone. But remember, when you meet them, **be with them**, spend some valuable time getting to know them!

2. Turn Yourself Off From Other Distractions Around You!

That also includes turning your mobile phone off or to silent mode. This will be really challenging for most people as you all love your incoming messages and calls—makes you feel wanted, doesn't it? Makes you feel important, doesn't it? Makes you feel good, doesn't it?… But what about the person whom you are with at the time?

When you are chatting on the phone or texting messages to someone else, the person you have just met knows that you are not focused on them. They would consider that to be a sign of ignorance or even worse, arrogance and non-interest!

A question I often get asked is, "What if they start using their phone and start texting?" Well, that's because you haven't got their attention yet and that's your fault! However, in first meetings, when the rapport is only just beginning, I would recommend you get on your phone at the same time as them, or do something else but let them know you'd like to continue your conversation with them after. Don't just stare at them using the phone.

You have to EARN THE RIGHT FOR
THEM TO PAY ATTENTION TO YOU!

This is just good manners, and do you know what? It is rare that people do what I've just shared with you. It is unfortunately not the commonly done thing right now as our lives move so fast, or more rightly put, we have allowed so many things to readily distract us. But courtesy and respect are the building blocks of excellent relationships, relationships of tremendous value, relationships that could build **more income** and a better life for you and them, as it can lead to many more opportunities!

Remember, the more quality relationships you have, the more opportunities you have to make a lot of money. It is precisely the quality of relationships you have that makes the difference between good and very successful, especially in sales where human interaction is a necessity. The more people who know how good you are, the more those people will recommend you and will want to join your community. Even if they don't buy anything at first, they will know others who will!

3. Never Assume Someone is Not A Potential Prospect!

The people you assume are not interested in what you are selling are the people that will potentially buy from you, you've just not asked them! The manner in which I am telling you this is that of the gorilla leaning back then leaning forward and banging both fists on the table in a frenzy!

Let me share with you this amazing story, something which happened to me when I first started in sales.

When I had belief, I didn't look at the customer and think, "Oh no, I'm wasting my time here, they'll never buy!" When I have belief, I assume that every prospect I have is a buyer!

One of my first sales was truly interesting because both of the prospects were blind! I only got to know it when I went to meet them at our reception. They even had their guide-dogs with them!

Many of my colleagues were cracking jokes with me before I started my presentation, saying things like, "They'll never 'see' the benefits, Marco!" which I admit was quite amusing at the time. However, I knew they could buy. I knew these people still needed to take holidays. (To refresh your memory, at that time, I was selling timeshare in Manchester—and the resorts were in Spain!).

All I had to do was make them see in their minds that they could really benefit from the product I was selling. And do you know what? They bought from me at the end and thanked me so much for not giving up on them, as all the other salespeople had done!

Interestingly, they became my best customers, came to my owners' gathering every week. And when they came, they brought their friends and told them how good I was and how good the product was! You can imagine my colleagues' attitude after this—they suddenly started looking for all the blind people they could find!

Another customer I had, I think it was my third sale—and I really have to tell you this because it also shocked me at the end—was a biker and his wife. The two of them had tattoos from head to toe! Plus, both had long hair, greasy, dirty-looking clothes and these huge biker-boots. I don't think there was anything else he could pierce. I mean he had metal rings all over his body, EVERYWHERE!

But what did I do? Well, I didn't assume. I just got on with the job and did the same presentation which I had always done since I found my belief. Two and half hours later, Alan, the guy, stood up out of his chair and started messing with his boots. Eventually, his wife, Carol, had to pull them off for him. No one in the sales office could take his or her eyes off this event—it was most unusual! He then shook his right boot over my table and something came out. It was, after counting it, 5,000 pounds! He then shook the other boot and another 5,000 pounds came out! Did I mind counting smelly money? Absolutely not! Their money was good as anybody else's.

You see, I closed because I did not assume. They liked me because everybody else had assumed. They told me how most people looked down on them. Alan and Carol became my friends for a very long time!

Question for you: How many times have you pre-judged a prospect by their looks? Go on, admit it!

Let's get one thing straight here. What I have shared with you does not mean I don't "qualify" my prospects. I will get to that later, but I certainly don't judge anyone by their looks!

4. Give, Never Take!

Always go into any relationship with the attitude, "What can I offer you?" not, "What can I get from you?"

I know we might be getting a bit ahead of ourselves here, but to truly focus on our customer's means they must be aware that you genuinely care about their needs and really want to get to know them. I'll be covering a lot of this in the next chapter when we talk about building rapport.

For now, let's learn how you can truly be a resource to your customer. They must know at the earliest opportunity that you are not a threat, and, most importantly, that you are not there to take anything from them! A common mistake among salespeople is asking for business too fast and trying to manipulate their prospects into buying something they don't know they need yet. Prospects will never buy from you unless they know you can be trusted, that you are totally focused on their needs, and you take the time to build a trusting relationship with them.

When you understand this, you have earned the right to close your prospect into a position where they will seriously benefit! This will cause them to take action and buy into the offering you are presenting.

By the way, most people believe that you have to take hours, days, and weeks to build that kind of trust. Not true at all!

If you truly are being yourself, have nothing to hide, and genuinely want to help your prospects, they will "see" that very quickly.

The reason they will see it quickly is because it's something they don't commonly see. Therefore, they will find you **extremely refreshing indeed** and will be attracted to you and your product or service because you have focused on them and ultimately shown interest in them!

Now, a quick recap of this chapter:

1. Value the opportunity to meet them!
2. Turn yourself off to other distractions around you!
3. Never assume they are not a potential prospect!
4. Give! Never take! What can you offer them, not what can you take from them!

And just to add one more thing—this goes to the guys first! When you see a beautiful woman, a woman so attractive that you would do anything to meet her, what do you do?

The guys know this, but I will tell you ladies, what a guy does when this happens: he will drop everything he's doing and focus completely on that woman! Nothing will distract him!

The same goes for the girls doesn't it? If you were to meet a really attractive man, a man so attractive that you lose all sense of self-control, you would drop everything! You want to focus on only him because you are so captivated!

The same goes with anything or anyone very important to us—our children, our partners, our way of life, etc. If you suddenly were to see something which would threaten or drastically improve your situation, you would **focus** on it with all your might!

That's what real focus is all about. If you take the time to seriously do that with all your prospects, you will be going to the ATM and celebrating every step you make!

CHAPTER 9

RAPPORT

"They must know you understand them."

What is rapport? Why is it critical to closing your prospects?

**Rapport is the level at which your customers
know that you totally understand them.**

There are so many misconceptions about rapport that it is really challenging trying to grasp what it's all about. Rapport is definitely not about agreeing with your prospects. It is all about how well you understand them and that they can see you understand them.

How many times have you heard the objection, "I'm just not interested, it's not for me"? The root of this objection is the lack of rapport you have with your prospect. There is no way they will respect you, like you, or indeed buy from you if you don't understand them. How could they?

They have to like you in some way to be able to trust you and give you money for what you are selling. They will only buy from you if they truly need what you are offering. Remember, I said if **they need it**, not if you need to sell it! There's a big difference. When you need to sell something, your customers will sense it real quick!

I remember years ago in an old-school training course I attended, the speaker said, "Imagine they've got a check on their forehead with your name written on it. All you have to do is find a way to grab that check!"

It is great, of course, to be able to get some focus, but the trouble with that is, you tend to forget to want to build rapport because you want the check so much! And this is where there is conflict between you and the customers.

Your customers will view your approach as desperate! And they would want to avoid it big time! They don't want to be sold something they don't feel they need! When you don't understand them, that's how they will feel!

A lot of great salespeople will know this:

The customers who seem the least interested at first and give you the most resistance are usually those who eventually buy from you!

Why is this so? Think about what I have just said. The people who give lots of resistance are actually communicating to you what they don't want and what they do want!

They are telling you HOW and WHEN to sell to them! They are doing everything to allow you to UNDERSTAND them first!

You see, this really is the pivotal moment in any sales career. It is the moment you understand that **resistance** and **objections** are really good and that you need more resistance to sell more products and make more money! It is the moment you realize that **resistance** is a very powerful feedback mechanism to help you lead them in the right direction, tailor and customize your sentences, syntax (order of the words you say), and more importantly, the questions you ask, and how and when you **listen** to them.

The most efficient way of overcoming resistance and truly understanding your customers' needs is to build rapport with them at the earliest available moment! And here's something you need to understand and think about. Let me ask you a simple question: who are the people you want to spend the most time with in your life?

You would say your family and friends, right? So what's the reason for that? Well, the reason is that your friends and your family understand you the best! I mean, the reason you call them your friends is something special to you, isn't it? You don't call everybody your friend! You call your friends the people who really understand you, listen to you, and are really concerned with your needs and desires. They travel the journey with you, supporting you in everything you do, even in your mistakes and through the wrong decisions and choices you make. They laugh with you at the stuff you've been through together and empathize with you when it's not going so good! Those are your true friends! That's why you have labeled them that way because they have earned it. Because they have taken the time to focus on you! They have taken the time to **rapport** with you!

But sadly, on average, most people at the time of death can't count their real friends on even one hand. We only count fewer than five worthy of that label!

**A champion salesperson is a GREAT friend,
and a great friend sticks around!**

It's that simple! All those qualities which your best friend has are what you should be demonstrating to all your customers! As with all great friends, you should be prepared to lead your customers to a place that's good for them, a place where they can see that buying from you would be a fantastic decision.

As I said before, you don't have to agree with everything they say. You just have to understand everything they say and show you understand by acknowledging it in some way, using your body language and voice. When your prospects know you "get" them, they are inspired to trust you more and tell you more. Then they begin to like you more! Not "getting" prospects is the one of the biggest, if not the biggest, mistake a salesperson can make in any engagement!

Milton Erickson, a highly accomplished and renowned hypnotherapist and a genius at building rapport, gives this example: One day he had a very upset client come in, telling him that she believed her life was finished. She was virtually suicidal. She felt this way because the perception of herself was dire— she thought she was fat and ugly, and totally believed that no one would ever love her. She was indignant; she wouldn't be moved from her opinion. The day she came into Milton's office she was a complete mess. She looked like a train-wreck, was not groomed, and was wearing an astonishingly hideous polka-dot dress!

So what did Milton do? He didn't offer empathy at all! He told her straight in the face that she was ugly and fat! He also told her a lot more things which were not complimentary! And guess what? He was **the first person** to have ever told her that!

A short while later, this lady made a miraculous recovery! She was all better and the reason she was better is because she felt that Milton was the only person to really "get" her! He told her the truth (that she needed to hear). There were no fancy names for her problems or empathy to try and get money from her. She said she had seen lots of therapists and they had all sympathized, but never "got" her. But because he "got" her, she was able to trust him very quickly. This allowed him to take her to a better place. She **trusted** him because he had a very strong **rapport** with her! Because of this, because she believed he was the only one to understand her, she "knew" he was the only one who could help her and knew how. True enough, he knew what she needed, and she bought what he gave her without question, without doubt, without fear—of making the wrong decision!

There is something you must know. Milton was not randomly talking with this lady; **he knew exactly what he was doing**. He knew what he had to do because he had successfully done it before. He knew what worked best and he knew the only way he could help her was to build rapport with her first! He put himself in her world and knew exactly how she was feeling!

By the way, if you think hypnotherapists, psychologists, and doctors are not salespeople, you are dead wrong! These people are selling everyday to "win new customers". Milton Erikson was a master salesperson!

Understanding your customer allows you to flow with your customer. It gives you an opportunity to harmonize with them!

So many salespeople have said to me: "What if I don't agree with them? I can't agree with them all the time! I don't want to lie. I want to be straight with them."

You have to understand that people think what they think and form their own opinions on what they have learned somewhere else. They will form their own perception of what you are offering them even if they haven't seen it yet! They will associate their previous experience with your offering to a similar experience they have already had with a similar product, maybe even yours! So your prospects will be showing you their interpretation or model of their own world—a world **that makes sense to them!**

Now, it may make no sense to you at all! And if it makes no sense to you, how can you possibly "get" on their level?

The thing is, you have to see why they think it makes sense to them, why they think your product does not suit them in their world.

Once you understand where they are coming from, i.e. you "feel" them, then you can really tune in to their psyche. You would really switch on to their needs since you can now really agree with how they feel and agree that you would feel the same way if the same thing happened to you. And you can do this without compromising your own opinions, values, or doing anything else that you consider lying!

Amazing isn't it, that so many of us just don't put any importance on this at all? And yet this is where we should be focusing most of our attention!

Simply put: Without rapport, there is no sale. When you have rapport, you can lead them to buy without ever having to close them! You just lead them there, because it makes sense to them! When it makes sense to them, they "get" what you are offering on an emotional and logical level. It would just feel like a natural thing for them to do. It is part of their buying process!

Moreover, it's not how fast you build rapport; it's how efficiently you build it. By efficient I mean you know what questions to ask, you know when to ask them, and you know when and how to really listen to them! You move closer to rapport when you have grasped the art of listening. Yes, you move to the next level of the game most efficiently when you apply EFFECTIVE LISTENING SKILLS. It is the quickest route from meeting them COLD to ending up establishing a valuable RELATIONSHIP!

There is no deal if there is no rapport! To the slower learners out there, that means there's no money going into your bank account! Have you really "got" this chapter yet? Or are you still stuck in the paradigm of how good your presentation should be?

Your presentation is all about how well you build the relationship; it's not about remembering every feature of the product! Prospects are not interested in how well you know your product; they are interested in how much you are interested in them. They want to know how far you are willing to go to **invest in the relationship** before you try and close them into the purchase—how far you will go to truly **understand** them!

Knowing when to close the deal is knowing as much about rapport building as you can, learning everything you can about it, to the point that you can execute it with ease!

This level of understanding of rapport building will ensure that you are always ready and aware of when to close the deal, and when to ask for the business! It'll ensure that the first thing on your mind before any meeting is doing everything you can to form an excellent relationship with your customer.

Many readers at this stage will be thinking, "My goodness, that will take so long! I don't have the time!"

Now that's a great point! I can see how you would feel that way if you just read to this point! I would too! (Getting it yet?) I will state here and now: it doesn't have to take long. It could only be five minutes—if you have mastered the skills! Remember, I said earlier, it is how efficiently you build rapport, not how quickly!

When you have mastered the learning process in this area, building rapport doesn't mean building rapport! It'll just flow from you naturally and people are attracted by that kind of authenticity.

Everyone loves people who are interested in them! This is an immutable, unchangeable fact! How well and genuine you show that interest in others will win you so many customers! That is how champions do it! They stick to the rules of success and always without exception, apply them with every single person they meet! Notice I didn't say prospect here. I said person, because everyone you meet can become a valuable customer of yours without exception!

In the next few chapters I will outline in detail the roadmap for building outstanding levels of rapport with everyone you meet. They'll be levels of rapport that make you loved and remembered with clarity by everybody you come into contact with, which means they will think of you clearly and powerfully whenever they need your advice, your services, or your products and you will be the first person they will recommend to their valuable contacts!

Here is a quick guide to building rapport.

1. Visualize and put yourself in the clients' shoes

What are their concerns? How are they feeling?

2. Mirror and match your clients' BODY LANGUAGE

Mirror. Look at your customer. Observe how he is sitting, and precisely what he's doing with his arms and legs and expression. Now attempt in a subtle way to imagine your client is looking in a mirror and he can see that you are in a very similar position. Move to mirror your customer's body language. This will put him far more at ease as it communicates that you understand him far better and you are sensitive to how he's feeling. If you do this well enough, you will see your clients instantly relax!

Match. Another effective technique is to match your client's movements. If are you sitting or standing next to him slowly and subtly move to match his posture and actions. For example, if his arms are folded, fold your arms. Or if he crosses his legs, cross yours.

Effective body language accounts for 55 percent of any effective communication! Use it!

3. Ask relevant, open-ended questions!

Questions which are open and require answers other than yes or no should be used at all times, especially when building trust. You must allow your customer to speak. They love the sound of their own voice. It also gives you the magic opportunity to listen!

4. Listen actively and intensely and focus

When you ask a question, it is how you listen and respond that will determine, categorically, to them if you are interested in what they are saying. If at any time during your relationship building they realize that you are not actively listening to their every word and syllable, you will not earn their respect and you will not build trust and rapport.

How you listen is the key to winning your customers' confidence and turning them into friends and clients of your company. Emphasis should be placed on this at all times.

5. Tone and voice structure

Tone accounts for 38 percent of your communication. When you are given the opportunity to listen and then respond to their communication, care must be taken to match the tone of your customer's voice. For example, if you have someone who talks very slowly and deliberately, a strategy of talking fast and aggressively will not be heard by this person. It will destroy any headway you have made in building trust.

A few components of tone to focus on are:

A few components of tonality to focus on are:

Loudness or Volume

Sharpness

Speed

Resonance

Tone

Clarity

Bass

Intonation

Softness

Pronunciation

Roundness

Annunciation

Congruence: Are you being genuine and sincere

If you don't believe in the product you are selling and you haven't learned your presentation well enough, your customers will definitely see that you are incongruent or don't really mean what you say. A lack of enthusiasm will be transferred from you to them. This will mean many things to your customer but most of all that you're not really interested in what you are doing and are lazy. Then they will have no respect for and will reject your offering.

BELIEF comes first; LANGUAGE is then inspired by your belief; ENTHUSIASM is expressed genuinely; CONVICTION then comes naturally; BELIEF is then TRANSFERRED to your customer.

Simply put, you must be sincere and match your language to your beliefs. When you do this, your body language will improve instantly and you will be most effective in persuading your customer to partake in your offering EASILY!

OPENING STRATEGIES

Get rapport and find their DBM (dominant buying motive, or the reason they will buy your product today)!

LOOK at the "stages of rapport" in the diagram below. Each and every one of those skills is necessary in creating phenomenal rapport and priming your prospects for your closing processes. I have dedicated one chapter for each of them.

Remember, you have to OPEN your prospects first before you can CLOSE them. When you have learned all those skills, you will know when to close the deal!

Speak in **people's** own language which they can understand. Create rapport. Then lift them to a place where "magic" happens!

"Give, never take! Always go into any transaction with what you can offer them, not what you can take from them!"
MARCO ROBINSON

STAGE 1. RAPPORT

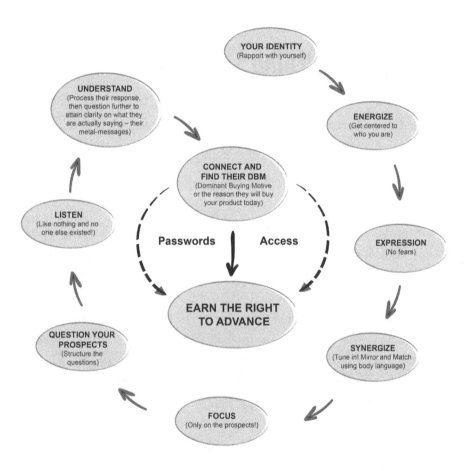

STAGE 2. RAPPORT

CHAPTER 10

STEP 1–YOUR IDENTITY

"Be yourself. Know who you are—your own identity, and rapport first with yourself!"

Let's get something straight here. This is not a book about finding out who you are. It's too huge of a subject to cover here, but I will recommend further reading on it as it is imperative that you do know yourself and you are able to be yourself.

It might seem strange that I said "rapport first with yourself" but there is a relationship going on inside you or you wouldn't exist!

I know you talk to yourself—we all do! We have to do that to be able to think and process information. If the normal conversation in your head goes something like, "I don't like this job. I don't trust my boss because he's a b*****d, and this product, I don't know whether it's right, you know... Maybe I should stay in bed today, I really can't be bothered prospecting. God, it's so hard! Why does it have to be so hard? Why can't these products sell themselves? Am I really doing the right job? Perhaps it's not for me. I don't think I'll ever make it sales, it's just not me!" Then you are really in big trouble!

You and I know we have had those conversations in our heads! That little conversation above would have sabotaged any success you might have had and would not allow you to create rapport with your customers. When you have not aligned yourself properly, you will be blocked at an emotional level every time you attempt to communicate with your customer, because you don't feel like it! Of course you can try and hide it, but you will be unsuccessful in doing this unless you change the conversation in your head!

Here's a great one! "I feel really fantastic today. I just know I'm going to have a great day and I know, I just know, definitely I will close some sales! I just feel in that mood, you know. I just feel so good I don't care what my prospects say, I don't care if they give a thousand objections. I'm actually really looking forward to the challenge! Wow, I've got goose-bumps!"

Which conversation is more empowering? Do you think I write these things down lightly? Which conversation do most "salespeople" have with themselves?

CHAMPIONS don't allow that negative first conversation to take place. They recognize from a very great distance the damage that would cause to their success. They block it! Average salespeople don't have that discipline. They allow those "negs" to occupy their minds for far too long until they cause a disease of inaction and failure!

Let me reiterate. Get the rapport in your head positive and empowering. Feel good about yourself. Know you have the ability to be a champion closer or don't even bother "trying" to build rapport, because you will fail!

Fear disappears when you have mastered the necessary skills.

If I could tell you in a few short lines how to do this I would say to you: To grow and improve, you have to feel fear. As soon as you have mastered what you need to learn, the fear will disappear—as if it was never there in the first place!

It comes down to this: Repetition is the mother of all learning! Once you speak empowering words that build your self-esteem, such as, "I know I can do it, I have the ability, I can conquer my fear, I can close the deal, I am confident, relaxed and in tune with myself," you will be able to do what you need to do without worrying about failure.

Confident people know they will make mistakes all the time. However, they also know they have the confidence to correct those mistakes, because those mistakes are making them learn, grow, and get to a better place, where ultimately and automatically they will get better results.

Remember the first few chapters? Be the HERO, take the journey, and know it will happen. If you hear any negative words or sentences in your head at any time, know you are taking the role of the victim as soon as you acknowledge them!

It is critical, that in those moments of making mistakes and failing, you have a MENTOR beside you, someone who can point out your errors and blind spots in case you don't recognize them (because habits become unconscious actions).

One of the most powerful learning lessons I had when I was failing in sales was having my mentor come with me on an appointment to see how I was doing it. That first debrief with him after my presentation was absolute gold, because I was suddenly aware of the mistakes and knew, for the first time, why my clients were responding negatively. Then I became more competent and effective, and eventually became a mentor myself.

Getting yourself mentored is going to make you a lot of money!

That's why I always, always, always, insist you carry this book around with you at all times and refer to it. Use it as your instruction manual and if you have questions or need to clarify any concerns, just come to the website and join our fantastic community of champion closers, where you will feel uplifted by the company you keep!

CHAPTER 11

STEP 2—ENERGIZE

"Get into your most powerful state!"

To effectively achieve any task at hand, we need to be in the right state. What kind of state do you think is needed to enable you to start closing more sales? Obviously a state that empowers you to be at the height of your "powers" when you get started!

Let's call this a PEAK STATE. A peak state is the opposite of a weak state! A peak state is when you absolutely feel at the height of your powers, when you feel wonderfully connected, when you have no thought of sleep, no doubts, and you feel energized and prepared for any event, good or bad! It's the kind of feeling you get when you've just closed a big deal. One that took you a lot of effort to get, so much effort that the celebration you make after lasts just as long as getting the deal in the first place!

I'm sure you know what I mean. Your customer just said yes. Shook your hand strongly and smiled. You smiled. Your whole body buzzed, and you've got goose-bumps again! You feel so good that you are jumping up and down on the inside! But you can't show it yet as you want to make it professional for your client. So, when you have got the deal all tied up and the money in place, you excuse yourself for a little "toilet break". You close the door, bring your arms up as high as you can and bring them both down in such a powerful move that you feel your muscles on fire! You tighten up, and say "Yes!" or "Yes, Yes, Yes, Yes, YES, YES!" while walking around the bathroom. Yes, just like the "victory dance" football players do when they've scored that vital goal or touchdown! That feeling, my friends, is why I'm writing this book. I still get it now. It's just the same even after 20 years of selling!

I guess I'm in the right vocation! You know that when you can celebrate the way I've just described. It's just awesome to feel that kind of energy. It's why you do what you do! And then you get the recognition from your peers and bosses. The pats on the back and the, "You did a fantastic job on that one!" kind of statements.

Sometimes the recognition is so good that it feels like you are on American Idol and have just inspired Simon Cowell to get up and give you a standing ovation!

How would that make you feel? Well, I'll tell you: there's not much better!

Now here's the interesting thing:

Champion closers feel like that before they close the deal!

Just in case you didn't get it, let me repeat that. Champion closers experience their peak states before they close the deal, during the presentation. They even feel in their peak states when their client says no, because they use that as a signal or signpost telling them that they are closer to the next YES!

They know they are following their true path whether they are rejected or not. They also know that as soon as they let go of that beautiful state, they will let go of their success, because they go hand in hand!

These are ingrained habits champion closers learn, because they know what works and they only SERVE what works for them.

Let me reiterate. Get into peak state before you see your client. If you are slipping out of your peak state, recognize that and get back to where you should be!

You're probably asking now, how in the world are you are supposed to get into your peak state when your ATM card has just been eaten by the machine!

Use this moment to be grateful that you're BROKE! It'll give the champion in you the DESIRE to make money!

Champions use that predicament as a positive blessing. They would spend all their time finding their peak state which they had obviously lost.

Champion closers do not have problems generating cash fast. Let me repeat that for you in a different way.

Champion closers can find the cash they need within the same day they have the cash shortage!

Why? Because they know what they have to do and who they have to be to make that happen! And they don't hesitate for a moment, because hesitation is not a champion's habit—it's a loser's habit!

Champions do it and love the process of doing it no matter what the obstacles. Losers don't do it because they are afraid the process will make them fail. If you read the last sentence again, you'll probably realize how stupid it is to be a loser!

Getting into Peak State

I've actually shared with you how to do this above. Let me put it down in three simple points here.

1. FOCUS and rehearse the presentation in your mind and VISUALIZE yourself being successful. Ensure total clarity. See the moment in

bright colors! Visualize that movie getting bigger and bigger and kind of enveloping, so that you are actually in your own movie. See the expressions of your customers, the delight in their faces when you share with them a benefit!

2.   MOVE your whole body as though you are celebrating closing the deal. Read again what I said earlier, about that feeling you get when you get that goal. Say out loud, "Yes, Yes, Yes, YES!" Keep saying it until you feel it!

3.   COMMUNICATE with yourself. Tell yourself the words you need to hear, the words that energize you, e.g., "Yes, I can do it! I'm going to do a fantastic job today! I'm going to make a lifelong friend of my client! I'm going to change their life! I know they will thank me for helping them and that will make me feel totally unbelievable!"

Before you start thinking, "Golly, that's going to take me hours," let me tell you, champion closers can go through that three-stage process in seconds and still get to their peak state!

I'm only showing you the way. If you believe it's not important to get into a peak state, or you feel too embarrassed and think it's a waste of time, then there's no way on God's earth that you'll know when to close the deal and suddenly grow rich! You will remain a loser, a broke loser.

And I don't use the word "loser" lightly. If you believe in God, you know that He will only help you if you help yourself. And He wants you to celebrate and be in your peak state at every opportunity!

It actually takes very little energy to do what I've just shared with you. It'll eventually become a habit which you love, because you will know that it's an essential ingredient to your continued success.

CHAPTER 12

STEP 3—EXPRESSION

"Broadcast Yourself!"

O nly after you have achieved stage/step 2 above can you then broadcast! Your communication must come from within. It must express the feeling that you care sincerely. Don't be a fuzzy TV! Let people tune in to you by tuning in to yourself. Your broadcast should come from within yourself—not from the outside! Take away the interferences. Be clear, transparent, and beautiful!

Compare yourself now to the TV. This is what you watch most of the time. How other people "see" you depends on your internal broadcast.

- Brightness = (energized)
- Contrast = (variety)
- Color = (content)
- Sound = (voice quality)
- Sharpness = (clarity)
- Depth = (character)

Your old broadcast has made you as successful as other people have seen you! By the way, we are always broadcasting, like it or not! If others see a fuzzy picture when you are broadcasting, they will not see success. And once they don't see success, they will not want to attach and connect themselves with you.

So expression is all about how you feel inside. That means you can only express yourself; therefore, who you really are! You can only express yourself at that given point of time. If you are not feeling good or not in your peak state, that is exactly what you will broadcast to your customers at that time, therefore be very aware of how you are coming across to your customer. It can seal or break the deal.

**That's why knowing yourself always comes first,
being yourself second, and expressing that self third.**

When meeting a customer you have to ask this question:

**What state do I need to be in right now
to effectively make the right impression?**

Losers won't be able to answer that question, but champions can flick a switch in their minds and suddenly be an astounding resource to their prospects.

**In an instant, champions will switch from "intra-personal
communication" (talking to yourself) to "interpersonal
communication" (talking with the prospect).**

The person who's still talking to himself when he's with others will not be able to build rapport with other people. Why? Because he's already busy with someone else—himself (or herself)!

In summary, to express yourself fully, you must RELATE to your prospects immediately when you start any communication with them. If you don't do this effectively, they will perceive that you are not focused on them and therefore don't care about them. You will have no chance with them!

Flick the switch and express that champion broadcast. Be bright, have clarity, and relate!

CHAPTER 13

STEP 4—SYNERGIZE

"Tune in by Mirroring and Matching Your Prospects"

Try this little exercise: The next time when you are engaged with a prospect, imagine they are looking into a mirror at themselves, and you are the person they are looking at. Now move your body very subtly (so they don't notice) so that your body is a direct reflection of theirs. That means you are seated or standing exactly like them as though they were looking into a mirror.

When you have accomplished this, you will notice that your customer will literally move into a different position and start to look a little more relaxed than they did just before you did this. This happens because when your body's movements begin to complement theirs, they are subconsciously being flattered by your mirroring technique. Because their self-esteem is increasing, they will subconsciously begin to like you more.

Whoa, you say! Yes, I'm telling you a fact in body language strategy that is incredibly effective and essential in building rapport.

You see, by mirroring them, it is as though you are understanding them, because you are showing you are in the same place they are, so therefore you "must" understand them! If you were to read back to where I mentioned about the genius of Milton Eriksson, about how good he was at always relaxing his clients, showing them that he really "got" how they felt, that he really understood them, etc., well, this is what you are doing now!

You are "understanding" them, and they love you for it, because they start to feel better about themselves!

This amazing technique is not so shocking when you realize that non-verbal communication accounts for over 90 percent of your success in sales. Yes, non-verbal, meaning body language and tone (the way you say things), not the words you say!

PROXIMITY

Something else you must focus on during any communication is your proximity to the prospect. Please note this is a variable. You need to be constantly aware of this and adjust to suit the best distance between you and your customer!

People's sensitivity to their own zoning or territory is crucial in the art of rapport. An individual's zones change all the time depending on:

- Expectation
- Individual
- Mood
- Masks
- Masculine/Feminine polarity energy
- Environment
- Circumstance
- Attraction: chemistry
- Familiarity: what do you know about the other person?
- Behavior: values demonstrated
- Physiology: body expression
- Impact on the senses

—Proximity Zones/Distances—

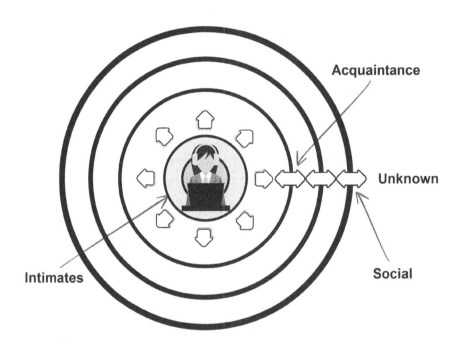

Tone and Voice Quality

Synergizing is also about your tone and the pitch and tone you use when you are asking questions and responding to your customer. This does not mean words. Remember, I mentioned that 90 percent of all communication is non-verbal! This is about how softly or loudly you speak, how fast or slow you speak, how you use your emotions when you speak, and how you use empathy in your tone!

If you are not sensitive to this and you speak too loudly while trying to engage someone who speaks softly, for example, you will literally scare your prospect away! He will adjust his proximity to you or, worse, make an excuse to leave!

Question them. Ask a few "surface-level" questions. See how they respond. Hear them then adjust your tone accordingly. If they talk slower than you, don't talk as fast as you normally would—but don't make it that obvious. If you copy them exactly, they will feel you are deliberately trying to know them "too much", that is, they will feel that you are trying too hard, which means to them, you must be desperate! That, of course, is a no-no. There is a balance and you will find it!

CHAPTER 14

STEP 5—FOCUS ON YOUR CUSTOMER!

"Never, ever let them 'see' you are distracted!"

W e've already covered this at length in previous chapters, but it is now that you have to really execute this skill in full.

Synergizing allows you to "tune in"—adjust that radio dial so you can clearly hear, see, and understand everything your prospect does. In fact, once you have had enough practice, you will become so skillful and good that you will be able to see a "pattern" in every person with whom you speak. You will start to recognize very early in the conversation what kind of "buying personality" a prospect has by his behavior.

This "pattern recognition" will allow you to "fine tune" and "calibrate" your actions to achieve a peak state of communication and set yourself up to have the best opportunity of closing your prospects in something they really want as soon as possible. Why delay closing if they really want it?

And the bonus is your prospects will love you for doing this! They respect you a lot more when you are able to fully focus on them. It boosts their self-esteem to such a degree that they will want to spend more time with you. They will be attracted to your personality subconsciously, because every time you spend time with them, according to them, you focus on nothing else but them! When you are truly aware of this critical process, your sales will literally soar! You just have to practice it!

However, be prepared not to be distracted by anything or anybody else other than your clients, which I am translating to:

- No phone calls during the presentation
- No sms (text messages) social media posting, browsing, either!
- No looking at girls or guys who walk or drive by
- No looking at your watch
- No thinking about negative loser thoughts such as your own problems
- No rushing to the next appointment

You can only ask them to focus on you and turn their phone on silent when you have earned the right, and you can only do this by focusing on them!

CHAPTER 15

STEP 6—ASKING QUESTIONS

"Learn the art of getting your prospects to speak more than you"

To listen effectively to your clients and truly understand them, you must go through the QUESTIONING PROCESS throughout your presentation. Question them, listen to them, clarify what they are saying, question again, and repeat the process again and again. These are the building blocks of building great rapport!

When you focus, you will gain a "sixth sense" of exactly what questions to ask them at that moment! I will focus another part of this book on the exact "syntax" of the questions, i.e. the order of words in your sentence. For now, understand that questions used for building rapport are special questions specifically for that purpose.

You do not use the same questions to close your prospects. You would use closing questions (which I will show you later), because to close you must open first—you can't close a door if it's not open in the first place! So building rapport is all about OPENING your prospects and finding the code to unlock their defense mechanisms, and there will be defenses, you can be sure about that!

Customers will not buy anything if they are not open to you. If they are closed up in any way, it means you haven't found the code to unlock them, i.e. you haven't found the right line of questioning! Or in the language of today… you need to discover what Algorythm they are running on and tune in.

There are two categories of opening questions. When asked at the right time and in the right way, these questions will synergize your communication and pull the prospects into your circle of influence. (Read Section 4 to know what questions to ask and when!)

Level 1 (Open): Connects (Finds Commonality)

Level 2 (PSYCHOPEN): Discovers (Finds Needs) and connects at a deeper, more powerful level.

How you listen to their answers is the key to unlocking their trust! (Refer to the next chapter.)

The Level 1 type "open questions" will commonly not unlock their buying cycle, because these questions are not meant to discover people's dominant buying motive (DBM) or the real reasons prospects need to buy your product. To really get to their decision-making, they have to feel it's good for them, and they only get that feeling when you have created a true desire for your offering.

You have to get to their subconscious mind as fast and efficiently as you can. Remember, they have to see themselves benefiting from what you are selling.

So the first line of questioning is really focused on building a connection with them, a commonality, something you can talk about together without having long gaps in your conversation. They are only going to buy or unlock their subconscious mind if they trust you!

Remember, build trust first. Don't ask the Level 2 "PSYCHOPEN questions" before you have attained a certain level of trust. You will know when you have trust. You will recognize it and then you can use the Level 2 questions.

What builds trust most effectively is listening to them after you have asked the "open" question, this is when they know YOU understand them! It's very easy to do this when you have the effective tools in your toolbox and it's easy to differentiate yourself from other salespeople as most salespeople fail to listen and fail to earn trust because the prospect is not sure they fully understand them!

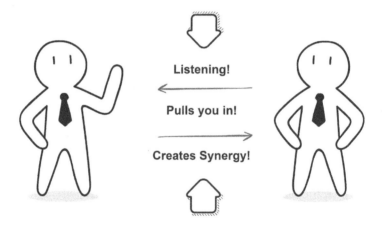

SECTION IV

THE TOOL-KIT TO
SUDDENLY GROW RICH!

CHAPTER 16

THE OPENING QUESTIONS—LEVEL 1

"Earning trust!"

As mentioned in Chapter 15, Level 1 questions are really about initiating a connection and finding commonality between you and your prospects. These questions are meant to help you find grounds for mutual liking and respect.

By saying commonality, I don't mean that you have to say that you also play golf if it's not your thing. Just a show of interest in golf will do. If you said you hated golf instead, it would destroy rapport and any opportunity you have. A commonality can mean you have the same passion about sports or doing something you enjoy in the sunshine. The experience can be the commonality.

If you said you play golf but really don't, sooner or later you're going to get caught. Yes, some closers are very clever at lying, but that is not my recommendation. The last thing you should do is resort to deceit at any time!

Building rapport is **understanding** why your prospects play golf, even if you hate it. They must do it because it gives them a certain experience and feeling.

All you have to do is **discover why they play**. This will give you an insight into what makes them tick, by knowing what they enjoy.

BIG Lesson

Get them on their favorite subject. Get them talking about them, because **most people's favorite subject is themselves!**

Opening questions are the only way you can do this. You **must** practice opening questions **before** you can close them. It is always far more effective to close them when they have responded to your opening questions.

Another BIG Lesson

Love and connection. One of the basic human needs is to connect with others. Connection with others makes us feel good about ourselves. It makes us feel alive and needed. It makes us want to open up and share our deepest feelings. This leads to our subconscious mind and our buying mechanisms. When a champion closer asks the correct questions, they "compel" his prospects to open up and connect with him and be open to connecting to the product he is offering.

If there is no connection, the prospect has not opened up and the product will be "compromised". What I mean is that whatever product you are selling will be "tainted" by you. Your prospects have to buy you first, not the brand! They have to connect with you first. They have to know they are not making a mistake. They have to trust you and therefore your recommendation to buy the product. They will buy if you can connect with their inner feelings and demonstrate that their life will be better by subscribing to your offering!

Here's a little manual on our first level opening questions.

Open Connect Questions—Level 1
Who; What; Why; How; Where; When

If you asked me where most salespeople **fail** when attempting to close any sale, it would be the absence of asking really great opening questions, i.e. questions that require the prospects **not** to answer yes or no!

If a prospect is answering yes or no to you all the time during your presentation, it can only mean you have not built rapport. You are not getting the opportunity to **listen** to their answers!

Remember: Asking an opening question helps the prospects build their self-esteem because you are listening to their answers!

Always, always remember "rule number one": **Get them to talk! Don't talk to them!** Here are some criteria and reasons for opening questions.

1. They are designed to involve the clients in the presentation, therefore to get them talking at least half of the time.
2. They are meant to gain information from the clients so that you can adapt the presentation to their particular needs: "working on their agenda"!
3. Any person's favorite subject is themselves! People love to talk about themselves once you start showing genuine interest in them. Only then will they start to like you!
4. People will not listen to you for two hours. They will mentally and emotionally switch off and break their nose on the table! Remember, "two ears, one mouth"!
5. It is better for the clients to tell themselves the benefits rather than the salesperson. They will sell to themselves if you ask them enough open-ended questions. Examples of these are:
    *   How was your day today?
    *   What kind of activities do you enjoy in your spare time?
    *   What do you love about your work?
    *   When do you normally go on holiday?
    *   Why did you choose to live in London?
    *   Who do you think highly of within your industry?
    *   What did you get up to today?

These are obviously not deep, but very surface-level questions. Remember, you cannot ask deep questions (Level 2 "super open" ones) until you've had many chances to listen. The above are not fantastic sexy questions. They are just "common" questions which you will ask. They become sexy only **when** you ask them in the right way, show interest when you ask them, and use the correct body language and mirroring techniques!

Let's work on the question "Why did you choose to live in London?" (You wouldn't just blurt this out. You would already know of course they lived there before mentioning "London"!) Now, when you ask, nod your head and prefix the question with something like, "**If you don't mind me asking**, why did you choose to live in London?" And you would say this with a lovely tone that shows you **are very interested**!

Why do I say this? Because most people ask these questions like they are doing a survey! They just run their mouth like a motor just because their boss has taught them this "sales technique".

Earn the right to probe!

Showing your interest and listening to their answers as I have said many times will earn you the right to probe their answers so you can get the information necessary to close them later. Think of it as "foreplay"! You and I both know sex is not good without foreplay. Sexual intercourse is best initiated with a series of strokes and mutual appreciation. It is the same in sales! And don't ever forget that!

You can't sunbathe if the sun doesn't shine and you are cold! Once you have asked these questions correctly, based on their answers, then you can probe.

JAKE: If you don't mind me asking, why did you choose to live in London?

PROSPECT: Well, the job really, but of course I love the energy of the city, the night-life is fantastic, and you meet so many interesting people here.

JAKE: I know exactly what you mean. The energy is kind of addictive, isn't it? Tell me, what is it about the night-life you love?

Take note that Jake has listened to the prospect, but he hasn't asked about his job yet. This is because obviously at this point in time, the prospect is not interested in talking about it by the way he dismissed it in the beginning. What Jake has done is first of all focused in on the fact that the prospect loves the night-life. Remember to get them talking as much as possible about what they **love**.

It's simple common sense that people are going to talk about what they are passionate about more because of their great interest in the subject. If Jake had honed in on the job topic—because Jake had been trained to get information about his prospects' occupation as soon as possible—that would not have been the best line of questioning, because that's not the customer's **hot** topic right now in this conversation!

Ask **more** questions about what they are interested in! This will open them up because they will be talking about their passions and things that interest them! Hence they will be talking with their feelings!

**They are compelled to connect with you
when you have unlocked their passions!**

Let's continue the above conversation a bit more and see where we go.

PROSPECT: It's just that you can basically do anything you want to do. I mean, one minute you can be in a normal pub, the next you can be a nightclub gambling, the next having a lap-dance, the next meeting some very unusual people. And on top of all that you can see the most amazing show on the west-end like Phantom of the Opera!

JAKE: Whoa, you sound so excited when you talk about that, it sounds like an amazing night out! I think I'd like to try that myself, but tell me, out of all that night-life, what's the one thing you'd say you enjoyed the most?

PROSPECT: Phew, all of it really… but I suppose meeting new people that are interesting. I mean, I just love connecting with people, you know.

JAKE: I do as well, so much! Isn't it fantastic when you do meet someone you connect with immediately? It's like bumping into an old friend, isn't it?

PROSPECT: It is, yes, it feels great.

JAKE: So tell me, who was the most interesting person you met when you were going out in London?

PROSPECT: Oh wow, there are so many… well, I did meet this stripper last week who has a doctorate in psychology!

JAKE: That's incredible! Why was she strip-dancing?

PROSPECT: Well, that's the interesting part! She said she wanted to know why men could get so distracted by a total stranger dancing seductively, even though she knew it was obvious, she wanted to know more. She wanted to get inside their thinking, and one of her biggest discoveries was, it didn't matter how happy or sad they were or even what they did for a living, I mean politicians, lawyers, all sorts of professional people were doing, that's what she couldn't believe at first! And then she wrote a paper on it—and got an award for her work!

JAKE: Holy cow, and I thought strippers were not intellectual! How wrong I was! It must have been fascinating to meet her, do you have her number? Hee, hee….

PROSPECT: No, but I know where she works!

JAKE: Good enough! I'll definitely try and get there the next time I'm in London.

At this point in time, I know what you're thinking: why the hell is Jake showing so much interest in strippers? You may be thinking he is wasting time and is going off-course! You know what? Most average people would think that!

But champion closers know this is part of the process and you must go through this connecting session. Even if it's totally unrelated to your presentation, that doesn't matter, because what matters is that **Jake is connecting with his prospect!**

And his prospect will like him for doing that. Why? Because Jake is showing interest in him and his way of thinking. Jake is complimenting him!

> **This "connecting" stimulates familiarity and relaxes the prospect! A relaxed prospect is a prospect with a lowered defense system and an open mind!**

When you have connected, then you can lead the prospect to the next stage and the next phase of questioning, i.e. the questioning that leads to discovering the DBM (dominant buying motive) or the main reason the customer will buy today!

Before we get into that, I think it's about time we well and truly covered the subject of **LISTENING**! Are you ready? Great! Pay extra attention to the next chapter!

CHAPTER 17

LISTEN!

"Shut your mouth!"

Okay, before we continue with QUESTION—LISTEN—CLARIFY— CONNECT, let's get very clear on the rules of listening!

Understand—Acknowledge—Agree—Clarify—Never Interrupt!

1. Always Understand First!

That's right, you know this now. Stephen Covey was right: "Seek first to understand!" Don't just let them speak, **focus** everything on understanding them first, i.e. **why** they are saying what they saying!

2. Acknowledge Everything They Say!

Although this is such a simple thing, many average, so-called salespeople fail to do this. You must acknowledge them, which is the opposite of ignoring them. Remember, by acknowledging them you are validating what they say, which makes them feel important and special! Acknowledge them by **nodding** your head, maintaining eye contact, and expressing yourself in relation to what they are saying. So if they share with you something surprising, **act surprised**! If they are whispering a secret to you, whisper back! Getting it yet? **Acknowledge them!**

3. AGREE WITH EVERYTHING THEY SAY (In an Understanding Manner)

Anytime you show you disagree with them, you will destroy any rapport you had. Agreeing doesn't mean agreeing with exactly what they say, such as if they said, "I don't like chicken," and you say, "I don't like chicken either!" What it means is, you would clarify first why they don't like chicken by saying, "Really, why is it you don't like chicken?" They may say, "Well, it gives me very bad indigestion every time I eat it!" So now you know the reason they don't like chicken, in which case, as you must understand and then agree, you would say, "Okay, you know what, I wouldn't like chicken either if it gave me indigestion all the time!" Do you see the difference? You don't have to say you don't like chicken first. You just have to understand why they don't like chicken! You are just **agreeing with the reason** they told you they don't like chicken. This is the science of true listening!

4. CLARIFY WHAT THEY SAY (So You Don't Make the Mistake of Structuring the Next Question Wrongly!)

If there's one thing that can blow your whole deal, it's demonstrating that you didn't listen to them properly because you didn't clarify properly! You clarify by saying to them, for instance, "So, what you are saying is, you don't like chicken because it gives you indigestion, it's nothing to do with its taste, is that correct?" You have to repeat what they said to you to actually clarify with them.

5. Never Interrupt Them, Ever!

Now of course, you could never repeat and clarify what they have said to you if you kept interrupting them! Interruptions will not only **destroy** any trust you may have had, but also make your prospects feel really bad and angry. They will feel this way because it appears you do not care about them, are not focusing on them, and are more interested in getting money out of them at all costs! When someone interrupts you, it is like your opinion is meaningless and has no importance, it makes you feel small and insignificant, and it **makes you close up**! And do you know what? It makes you want to **never** open up to that person again! So can you now see if you ever interrupt your prospect, you will have locked them up and thrown away the key and no matter what "opening" question you ask, they will not talk to you! **So, be very careful about this** as it could cost you dearly!

Everyone is guilty of doing this because sometimes the prospect says something to you that is boring, that you definitely don't agree with, or that is even insulting! That is the most difficult thing—to not interrupt—but there is always a very good reason they are insulting you or disagreeing with you. So your objective is to discover **why** they are doing that! And you can only do that by questioning them and listening to them fully so **you can understand why**. And yes, you heard it right, even if they are not nice to you, you must **listen** to them and let them **finish** what they are saying fully. In that way, they will eventually run out of steam and they will start to like you because you took the time to listen to them!

> **Clarity sets up the next line of questioning accurately.**
> **This is the true essence of this book—knowing when**
> **to listen, and knowing when to question!**

The tone and the construction of your next question will impact your buyer. You must analyze their response by listening with great intensity, then construct your next question based on their previous response—and listen again! It is an ever-increasing circle of energy. You will feel **great** energy in your communication when you have achieved this effectively, when you have found the **RIGHT WAVELENGTH**!

Let's look at a couple of examples:

If John asks you, "How was your day today?" and then doesn't wait for you to finish your response, that would destroy rapport or any opportunity of building rapport.

If however Jake asks you, "How was your day today?" and then waits for you to respond and really hangs on your every word and looks into your eyes, showing that he's really interested in your answer, that would build rapport and create more opportunities to build trust and a stronger relationship.

Do you see the difference? Jake listened and waited. How many people do you know who simply don't do that?

Even worse, some really bad salespeople will ask you one question, interrupt before you've finished, and ask a completely different question totally unrelated to the first or to your response! Do people actually do that? Absolutely, all the time, unfortunately!

For instance, if John asks, "How was your day today?" and then asks another question before you have finished, "Where do you live?" would this build rapport?

If Jake asks, "How was your day today?" and listens to you say, "It was good. I had a great game of golf and the sun was beautiful," to which he then asks, "How long have you played?"

Would you be more comfortable and relaxed with John or Jake? Who would you **open** up to more without feeling you were being interviewed or interrogated? Which of these two guys would you be able to create **MUTUAL ATTRACTION** or a mutual **LIKING** with?

Well of course it's going to be Jake, isn't it? Doesn't Jake make you feel better? Isn't Jake the kind of person you would tell your closest friends about and say something like, "I quite liked Jake, he was a really nice guy, I felt comfortable talking to him."

Now you wouldn't tell your friends the reason you liked Jake was because he let you finish what you were saying and he had great eye contact and so on. You wouldn't do that because Jake opened a little door to your subconscious and said hello, and you connected at a deeper level with him because **he actually was able to lift your self-esteem!**

Listening to your prospect builds their esteem!

Because he made you feel good, you didn't analyze it, you didn't think he was manipulating, you liked him! You didn't know why, you just did! And that, my friends, is the real **secret** of the **CHAMPION CLOSER**! The champion **knows** what to ask, when to listen, and what to say and when to say it and how and why he's saying it in that way!

Is that simple enough for you? I'm banging my fists on the table again: **Yes, it is very simple!** However, amazingly, average salespeople don't spend any time on this because they are desperate to close a sale. Therefore, they think spending more time on the closing and presentation phases is time much better spent!

Wrong! Yes, it would take Jake around the same time to connect with his clients that it would take the average salesperson to start the presentation. But it's not about how long. It's about focused questioning and listening—targeted at your **NICHE**!

Yes, **niche**. Your customer is your **niche** because every single one is different! You've probably heard that to be successful in selling over the internet you have to follow a niche and sell a niche product for a niche market! Yes, that's correct. It's the **same** for telephone and face-to-face sales, except the only difference is that these are dynamic. Meaning, you have to respond to your prospects' niche, i.e. how they respond and how they buy. Remember I talked earlier about each customer having his own buying cycle? Well, that is his own particular niche of buying.

> **So QUESTIONING is all about structuring the correct question for a prospect's particular response and catering to his niche buying cycle or the particular way he/she buys things.**

This is not quantum physics or splitting an atom. This is everyday common sense! I mean, come on, if someone says he had a great day playing golf, and you ask them where they live, would that be logical? Is that really constructing the appropriate question for his response? Were you even listening to him? Bottom line: *people will only buy from those whom they like*!

"People don't care how much you know, they care how much you care!"

Cliché maybe, but certainly true. Showing an interest in someone creates an attraction to you from that person. For further reading on this, I recommend you buy and read *How to Win Friends and Influence People* by Dale Carnegie. That is one of the best books you will ever read on how to improve your sales—besides becoming a better human being. It is timeless. The wisdom therein still applies today, and it is so refreshing when people use those skills because statistically, very, very, few do.

In that book, it says pay someone a compliment. Listen to Jake when his prospect talked about having enjoyed playing golf that day: "Wow that sounds really fantastic! I didn't know you were a golfer. It must be great to be out in the sunshine! Wish I could learn!"

Jake was showing interest and paying a compliment by saying, "Wow that sounds really fantastic! I didn't know you were a golfer...." It's not a direct compliment like, e.g., "You must be an awesome great golfer and I really admire that!" While that may be a direct compliment, is it genuine? Not really, it's too obvious. Jake would be trying too hard here.

"That sounds really fantastic" is better because it is subtle and sounds like Jake would really enjoy playing golf all day as well. It sounds like Jake doesn't have something his prospect has or had that day. That makes his prospect feels special because Jake has shown him that he admires the prospect having the time and the skill to do it.

Jake is the real genius here. You had better listen to him if you want to become a **CHAMPION CLOSER**. He will help you make millions! All because he knows how to question and listen effectively—a rare skill indeed these days.

BIG Lesson

When you ask a question, respond by listening first. Then carefully construct the next phrase and subsequent question accordingly to your prospect's niche. Ensure at all times you are focusing on your customer's interests, not yours. And, of course, never interrupt them—**ever**!

CHAPTER 18

THE DBM CODE CRACKERS—LEVEL 2

*"The DBM Code Crackers—discover
your prospects' true needs!"*

"If I gave you a million dollars and said you could only spend it on
your life insurance, what life insurance would you choose and why?"

Before you start thinking I'm selling life insurance to you, let's just study
the reasoning of the above question for a moment. I have used this
question and variations of it for different products and services for the
last 20 years. When it is asked at the right time, in the right way, with the right
level of rapport and harmony in the relationship, it will lead towards finding
the dominant buying motive (DBM) a lot sooner than if you just asked plain,
open questions.

What's the "DBM" or dominant buying motive? It's the main reason
your customer will buy the product today. That's right, your prospect has

to have a sufficient motivating desire for your product or they will not buy. Simple as that! Your job is to find this hotspot as soon as you can in your communication.

Think of yourself as a doctor.

When you go to the doctor, he'll ask you all sorts of questions to determine the nature of the problem you have, and only through asking questions does the doctor find the source of your ailment. Now if you can't answer his questions satisfactorily, he would have to get his knife out and start operating to "see" where the problem is!

You trust the doctor because he's the one who can make you feel better, and you co-operate by answering the questions he asks you. He listens intently; therefore, you have rapport. Your DBM is "get rid of the pain as soon as you can". Once the pain is gone, your desire to feel better is satisfied!

So just like a doctor, instead of trying to see inside a prospect's brain for his hotspots and desires, you must probe his psyche and ascertain his psychological needs regarding your offering. You can **only** do this effectively by asking **PSYCHOPEN** questions at the right time.

What's a psychopen question? Well, you won't find that word in the dictionary because I just created it, as I couldn't find a really suitable word to describe the kind of questions you need to ask.

A psychopen question is one that requires your prospects to give you a non-automatic answer.

It requires them to go deeper into their subconscious mind and retrieve answers that touch the center of their being and discover what they really want and need in their lives. It's a question they are not used to being asked. They are not used to being asked deeper questions because most salespeople don't ask those questions. They ask surface questions that the prospect can answer almost immediately in a kind of automated way.

For example, if I changed the question at the beginning of this chapter to, "What kind of life insurance would you like?", that would be a more surface-level question... although it appears to get the same answer. But would it?

Basically, the second question will elicit a far different answer than the first even with rapport. The answer would be more casual such as, "Don't know really, enough to cover the family in case I die."

That is not a great answer because it is not a great question!

So let's go back to the first question: "If I gave you a million dollars and said you could only spend it on your life insurance, what life insurance would you choose and why?"

The first part of this question is related to money, why? Well, one of the most common objections and concerns you will get in any presentation or pitch you do is the price. That means the prospect is going to start putting a price on your offering very early on. In fact, they will ask you the cost more times probably than any other question. Why? Because if it costs money and they buy it and it's **not** the correct product for their niche desire, they will have a made huge mistake!

Remember earlier in this book we discussed the main reason people don't buy your product is because they are frightened of making a mistake? It's true! The more money it costs, the bigger the mistake in their mind, or more accurately, their psyche. Their psyche includes their ego, and no one wants to hurt his own ego!

Tangibles and Intangibles

Sometimes, depending on the product or service you are selling, if it is tangible, something people can see and touch, like a mobile phone, computer, or car, your prospects will already know the selling price. This can be a good thing but it also can be a deterrent to making an appointment, because they already know how much it'll cost them.

In today's world, a lot of what we sell are "intangibles", meaning things that can't be seen or touched, like life insurance, software, training seminars, lifestyle experiences such as clubs and holidays, etc.

These are the products which the prospects will have to form pictures in their own mind of them using those products before they put **any** value on them.

That's why they will keep asking you, "How much is it?" They are just trying to grasp the concept you are offering with both hands and when they can't "get it", they become more afraid it's too expensive for them.

So when I begin my question with, "If I gave you one million dollars…" I am giving them the money first and therefore taking away the fear and objection of money. I am taking away the limitation of cost. Therefore the customer is more relaxed and open to really explore what they want their life insurance to be because they are free of the burden of thinking about the money. When you ask this question convincingly and at the right moment, the information you can gain is extremely valuable. Sometimes it'll be enough to discover their DBM and all their other hotspots, i.e. things that excite them.

The power of this question cannot be underestimated. I remember in a seminar I did recently, I had several insurance salespeople in my class. I offered this question to them to start asking on their next appointments. At first they dismissed it as silly, but none of them had ever used a question like that. They had assumed that all their clients wanted the same life insurance and they always offered the same packages, so I gave them a challenge.

I got two of them to ask the question I gave them on the next ten appointments and the other two to keep using the same questions they had always been asking. To ensure things went as planned, I went on five appointments with each group, posing as their trainee. To their great amazement, the two salespeople who asked the new question started to get different answers, and in three cases sold a package double the price of what they sold before. They also improved their closing percentage by 18 percent!

No way, I hear you say. Yes way! This really happened! And even more fascinating, when they got more confident in asking that question and asked more psychopen questions of a similar nature, their closing percentage improved even more!

**When you discover what your prospects really need, you can tailor
the perfect offerings for them, because they can "see" the benefits.**

The second part of this question says, "… and said you could only spend it
on your life insurance…"

So first I gave them the money which relaxed them. Now I'm qualifying that
money and saying they can only spend it on the product which I am offering.
This is useful because it gets them to focus on one thing and really get to the
psyche in terms of what they are really looking for, what they really want, if there
were no limitations.

This question will make them think and give you a non-automatic answer. It
will make them move their eyes!

The eyes have it!

Move their eyes? Yes, move their eyes! If you have ever studied NLP (Neuro
Linguistic Programming), you will know what I am talking about here. If you
don't, please allow me to simplify it for you.

The way people move their eyes in response to your question will indicate
what they are thinking about and what they are searching for. There are about
nine movements in NLP to look for, but I prefer to concentrate on only two of
them: #Eyes move up to their right, or #Eyes move up to their left.

Eyes Right

In my over 20 years of experience in selling and persuading, if the
prospects' eyes move to their right, they are accessing the creative right side of
their brain, thinking of an answer as it is unlikely they have been asked that
question before. They won't be used to it. There is no imprint of it in their
memory. They are searching for a creative answer. Could they be lying? It's
possible, but only if they look down generally. This is a fantastic response that
you really want because it gets them thinking and focusing on what you're
about to present to them!

Now, sometimes people's brains are wired slightly differently, meaning their eyes might move slightly differently as they access different parts of their brain, however generally any movement of the eyes in either direction is good because they are "thinking" more about the answer!

Questions that elicit non-automatic or non-reflex answers facilitate your prospect to focus more on you and your product.

An automatic, reflex question would be, "How are you today?" something which they have been asked so many times throughout their lives. When that happens, the answer is immediately retrieved from the conscious mind! But you don't want to get to the conscious mind. You want to get to the subconscious mind where the emotions and feelings are located.

Eyes Left

When your prospects' eyes move up to their left, generally they are accessing their long-term memory for a reference to answer your question, rather like going into an old filing cabinet and looking through the files! Once they retrieve a file or a memory that makes sense for your question, they will respond. Otherwise, they will shift right to look for a creative answer, as they can't find a suitable memory that matches.

In either the left or the right, you have a winning question because you have deeply **ENGAGED** your prospect. They will become less distracted and really start to focus on the conversation.

To give you a fantastic example of this kind of eye movement, watch what the contestants do on a quiz show. If they are not sure of the answer, their eyes will move to access the answers in their brains.

These questions also get the prospects talking more, which allows you more time to listen effectively to their responses. This builds **more trust and more rapport**! You can do anything **in** rapport, but nothing when you don't have it!

Never interrupt their thinking!

Remember I said never interrupt when they are talking to you? Well, I'm asking you now to take it one step further: **never interrupt when "they are thinking to you"! Stay quiet and pause** until they respond to you. If they don't respond to you, ask the question again until they do!

The weakest thing you can do as a salesperson is be afraid of the silence and keep helping them with the answers. This is closing suicide. It just won't work and it will make you talk more than them! Eventually you'll give up sales, because you're so tired—from doing all the talking!

Use silence and pausing as your friend!

I remember a few years ago I asked a closing question, which I'll talk about later, and I kid you not, we sat there for 15 minutes in total silence! I was waiting for him and his wife to stop thinking and make the decision. There was nothing else I could do and he knew it. So he sat there. He looked at his wife, looked at me, moved his eyes left and right. Then eventually his wife became uncomfortable and said to me, "What do we do now, Marco?" To which I replied, "Tell me if you would like it in one name or joint names."

"Joint names," she said, to which I then started the paperwork and processed the sale.

Silence is awesome. Never forget it!

The last part of the question I asked at the beginning of the chapter was, "… what life insurance would you choose and why?"

Now, literally, they could say anything here. They could say what company they wanted, if they wanted an investment, how much cover they wanted, their kid's education, just all sorts of things. Most times when I ask these kinds of questions I take it a step further and give them a list to choose from in their own minds. So the follow-up question, or the same question with a different ending, could be:

"If I gave you a million dollars and said you could only spend it on your life insurance, what three things must your life insurance have to make it perfect for you and your family?"

This small change helps them analyze the answer more effectively, because you have only given them three benefits to choose, so now they must prioritize. It is always best to ask this face to face and not in a survey because a survey is cold and people don't "think" to cold pieces of paper if they see no benefit.

So they might say:

1. "It's got to have enough cover for my family to never worry about money for the rest of their lives."
2. "It's got to pay out quickly and not wait years."
3. "It's got to have tip-top customer service. The one thing I hate about insurance companies is that is takes so long to get through to the person you want. I don't want to talk to a machine!"

By the way, these **are** the top three answers to that question out of all respondents! It's interesting to note the first priority is emotional. People care about their families. They don't want them to suffer. It's all about feelings first, or the deep psyche. This is the **real** DBM.

And why was price not here? Well, because I took away the price focus and objection that would normally have come along with this answer. Price was not on their mind.

People don't mind paying as long as they get what they want!

So from their answer, remembering to have listened to every syllable they have uttered with complete focus and interest, you can qualify a purchase with some test-closing questions. They could sound something like this: "So if your life insurance was able to perform to your needs and it was easily affordable, is that a company you would love to be associated with?

"That if your family never has to worry again, the service was fast, efficient, and personable, and it paid out within 60 days, guaranteed, would that be the most suitable life insurance for you?"

The first of these questions is simple and requires a yes, no, or maybe response. The second question repeats and clarifies what they have said to you, which demonstrates to them that you have been listening carefully, and this builds more rapport and trust!

When they answer, "Yes" to you, you know you are very close to their psyche and discovering their DBM. If they answer anything other than a yes, you have no rapport, they don't trust you, or they haven't been listening or thinking. This is your fault, so go back and get the rapport, with some more open questions. Don't keep asking closing questions again as this is forcing the issue.

**A closing question should come naturally,
smoothly, and conversationally, as a natural part
of the process. It should never be forced!**

So now that they have said yes to your test-closing questions, you can take it to the next level by asking them how they would feel if they owned that kind of life insurance. You can probe further and discover more—and get **them to tell you the benefits!**

**It is always better that your prospect tells you
the benefits of your product than you telling him!!**

Listen carefully to this because I'm only going to say it once! If you ever wanted a true signal that your prospect was ready to buy, there's nothing more powerful than your prospect telling you how good your product is! Yes, you heard it right: champion closers never really close their prospects. They get the prospects to sell to and close themselves! Why? Because…

**…whatever comes out of your prospects' mouths
they will believe or will want to believe!**

So when a prospect tells you how good your product is, he's selling it to himself and putting himself in the position of owning it. Pretty soon his credit card and checkbook will be on the table, ready to do the deal!

So the question is: **how do you get them to talk about the benefits? You ask them!**

Yes, there is no other way! You've already got a "yes" they would prefer that life insurance in their lives. Now you have to get them to own that idea, emotionally, logically, and psychologically. Here's a great question that elicits an **EMOTIONAL RESPONSE** and creates more urgency to buy **now**: "So how would you feel if you passed on and your wife and children could never pay the bills, and they were poor for the rest of their lives?"

You might be thinking this is a negative question, but is it? You are painting a picture of loss to your prospect, loss and suffering and scarcity. You are getting them to create a picture in their mind of their family suffering if they don't buy the right life insurance! Isn't that a fantastic positive question? Is it such a bad thing to sell something that will improve their circumstances and look after them should anything happen to them? Your questions are bringing life insurance to the top of their priority list. It's becoming emotional **and** logical to make the decision.

An answer from the prospect is usually something like this: "Well… I've never really thought about it. I suppose that would be awful, it really would.…"

Then ask them about the **FUTURE**: "Tell me five ways your life would change if you knew that whatever happened to you, financially your family would be secured for the rest of their lives, how would it help them?"

Although this, too, is an emotional question, it'll also allow your prospect to talk about the true benefits of owning your life insurance. (This question isn't just for life insurance, friends. It works on any product or service.) Again, the answer to this question will require your prospect to give you a non-automatic response and really start selling themselves.

"It would give me complete peace of mind, that's for sure. It would help me educate my children, fulfill their potential. I'd never have to worry again—wow, that would be something! It would offer security to my wife, in the fact that if she couldn't work, she could still live comfortably, lots of things!!"

Now let me ask you a question, friends. Would that question help you close your deal or not? How can you deny the power of these questions? They are going to make you a lot of money! They will make you a champion!

If you don't ask them, don't believe in them, or think they are silly, then you will get results that will keep you **not rich**!

Close The Answer!

You have now had a fantastic response, but can you leverage more? Yes, you can! Here's the perfect closing question to ask after this response from your prospect: "Can you now see why all my friends are buying this life insurance?"

This will give you **feedback** to tell you whether you are doing a great job or a loser's job. If you are a true champion, the prospect would answer this way: "Absolutely. I can see that very clearly. How much is it please?"

A loser's prospect's response would be: "No, not really. I'm not really interested in life insurance."

Huge difference, same question!

So what determines the different answer?

The level of rapport you have to gain complete trust!…
The level of rapport you have in the diagram below!

Look at the tone of the prospects' first response. They want what you are offering and you haven't even shown them the presentation yet! That, my friends, is a sign that you have asked some awesome **PSYCHOPEN QUESTIONS** and that you have learned how to **know when to close the deal**!

Study the diagram below and we'll move on to why you need to have credibility and professionalism when you presenting.

STAGE 2. RAPPORT

CHAPTER 19

BECOME AN AUTHORITY— OOZE CREDIBILITY!

"Once established, they will think of you always as their leading expert and resource"

According to the latest research by Carleton University, USA, it takes one-twentieth of a second for your prospect to form an opinion of you and an impression of you!

You will probably have heard somewhere that it used to take seven seconds. Well, today, as we have already discussed, everything is faster! Most people suffer from ADD (attention deficit disorder) and you are competing with so many more other salespeople and advertisements both online and offline! So prospects are going to compare you with a favorable impression in their mind with what you should look like to be able and qualified to discuss with them the product or service you are offering.

To become an established AUTHORITY, a "doctor" of what you do (as mentioned in the diagram in the previous chapter), there are two impressions you need to create:

1. **A solid great first impression**
2. **A solid great lasting impression.**

If you fail at both or one of these, your competition will easily beat you to the punch and capture the income and market share you failed to capitalize on. People need to know for sure you can be trusted and, just as importantly, that you can deliver what they need. When you achieve this, they will keep coming to you to buy your products and services again and again, because you have what they need and they know you can deliver.

In fact, this is so powerful that if you were their computer expert salesperson, as soon as they think of a problem, a need, or a desire relating to their computer, they will immediately form a picture of you in their mind! That is, they will associate anything to do with computers with you! It sounds incredible, doesn't it? But take a moment and think about it.

If you have a need for anything in your life, you will search for where to find it. Now if you don't know anyone in computers, the natural thing for you to do is ask your closest friends and family if they know anyone who does! And this leads to my second point: If your closest friends and family have a need for a new computer or any help with computers and you are aware of it, the first thing you will think about is your computer expert salesperson. You will think of him **because** you trust him and know that he can deliver and, more crucially, you will see no reason why your computer expert salesperson cannot help your friends in the same way he has helped you!

In fact, it will make you feel better and lift your self-esteem because you were able to help your friends and you know your friends will be very grateful to you. They will thank you and trust you more and bring you into their circle more because you have genuinely and effectively helped them. Your computer expert salesperson made a great first impression with your friends by filling their needs and solving their problems!

A great first impression and a lasting impression will improve your **income** and your **network**. It will also improve the **income** and **network** of your prospect! Why?

Because you were trusted and you delivered!

Well, how does one **gain the trust** of others? We have discussed asking questions and listening in the previous chapters. However, you can't deliver if you don't have that trust—they won't let you! So let's talk about that first impression for a start.

I. Creating a Solid Great First Impression

Prepare Yourself—Rehearse Yourself!

We shall discuss our dress sense in a moment, because that will be the first thing your prospects or contacts see! But when you start talking, they will very, very quickly—almost at light speed—be forming that impression of you. They will also be asking this question in their mind all the time: **"How can you help me?"**

If you can't answer that question to them subconsciously, you will never answer it consciously. The tone of your voice, as you now know, speaks to their very core and helps them decide if you are being yourself and if you are telling the truth, i.e. whether you are genuine. So be yourself at all times just as you learned in the previous chapters. And always be ready to answer their question clearly, confidently, and with complete clarity. The more questions you answer in that way, the better impression you will give your prospect.

Another question which you will have to answer very often is this: **"What do you do?"**

I can't begin to tell you how many people fumble at this. If you fumble here, you will be seen as lacking in confidence. That means they shouldn't trust you!

So give them a crystal pin-sharp image of what you do.

There has been a lot of advice over the years of your "elevator sales pitch", i.e. in 30 seconds or less you must tell them what you do and the benefit for them to get to know you better.

I don't know about you, but I have not been in many elevators where everyone feels comfortable in talking. An elevator ride makes everyone nervous because of the proximity to strangers. It's not exactly a place that encourages people—either you or your prospects—to open up!

So I don't meet people in elevators. I meet them at networking events, over the internet, and through referrals. It is at the precise time you meet them that you must be totally confident in your message.

So when someone asks you what you do at a networking event, what do you tell them? "What do you do?"

A bad response sounds something like this: "Well, errrmm… I work for this errrm… computer company and I errrmm… sell their products."

Does that sound familiar? Well, it should because it happens most of the time! You see, people are naturally shy at group events where total strangers abound. So their natural behavior is to "shy away" when they are forced on the spot to deliver. This, of course, is not what a champion closer would do.

A champion closer would embrace the event and embrace the opportunities! He or she will respond by saying, "I assist my clients' time and money by delivering customized computer and network solutions that enable their companies to surpass their targets every time. For a list of my clients and what they say about us, just go to our website."

When said with confidence and clarity, this answer can be extremely powerful. It will engage the other person so much that he'll be interested in knowing more. Why? Because the champion closer is not being pushy; he is not overselling himself or asking for business. He's simply informing the other person and giving that person a choice to visit his website. That means he is confident because he is not hiding anything. He is being transparent.

By the way, the buzzword in communication in today's market is TRANSPARENCY. That means people can see right through you and know what you do is good or bad. The fact that the champion closer is not hiding anything is very refreshing, and this attracts anyone to trust him and get to know him better.

Also, can you see the benefits the champion closer has given in just one sentence? You know, where he says, "I assist my clients' time and money...." What are the biggest things in business that companies are always trying their "darnest" to get more of and save more of? Yes, you've got it—time and money! So that hits straight at the prospect, that if the champion closer has saved other people time and money, he could also do the same for him!

This line oozes CREDIBILITY and encourages the prospect to ask further questions. Remember, if your prospect is asking questions, they are interested in you and what you do, but most importantly how it will benefit them. You will discover your prospects' dominant buying motive (DBM) far easier when they are asking you questions, not the other way around, because they are interested in you and you are answering their questions and showing that you care.

Your Appearance

When people first meet you, the first perception is everything. That one-twentieth of a second first impression is greatly assisted by how you are clothed and dressed. It really influences the prospect's view of you consciously and subconsciously!

You must dress yourself with care and consideration.
Cleanliness

One of the first things that strikes anyone meeting you is how clean you look and how clean you smell. Champion closers think about this at all times. That means they are aware about how clean they are constantly. For example, champion closers wash their hands a lot! In fact, people say to me all the time, "Why do you wash your hands so often?"

Clean hands are important to champion closers. **It signifies that you care about the next person you meet.** If people see you have dirty hands and nails and sweaty palms, they won't think it's pleasant shaking hands with you! It's something your prospects will remember vividly.

I shake hands with many people every day. Not all of them are clean. In fact, the ones that are clean tend to be the most confident and successful of the bunch. And yes, before you ask, I have measured this and found it to be consistent with all people I meet.

So clean your hands often. Don't just excuse yourself to use the washroom and then just go to the toilet. Go and wash your hands, with soap, and dry them! It'll make you feel really good and leave a professional impression with your prospects.

Your Breath

One of the things I come across often is bad breath. I have that experience most days of the week and, quite honestly, I just don't want to be around bad breath. It really makes me want to vomit! The smell is so strong that it completely takes over the meeting, and if either you or your prospect is not aware of how bad you smell, it's really unforgivable.

Always be prepared that you might have bad breath by buying a mouthwash and using it throughout the day, and a good quality mint freshener. This sounds so insignificant I know, but I can't emphasize this enough to you. The reason I feel so strongly about this is because of an experience I witnessed many years ago.

In a particular sales office I used to manage, prospects were invited through a telemarketing system. There were around 30 tables in that office and on weekends it would buzz with activity.

On one particular table, I noticed the prospects were not happy, and were asking to leave. As manager, I went over to their table to learn why they felt this way. On learning that I was the manager, the man got up from his seat and said he needed to talk to me in private.

When we were in a quiet space he said he could no longer sit on that table because the salesperson's breath was so bad and he just couldn't breathe that air anymore. He asked me if I could change the staff and give him someone who smelt professional! Of course, this was embarrassing, but I learned something that can be paramount in successfully closing the deal.

I went back to the table with him and "smelt" for myself the unwanted odor and quite rightly, it was not pleasant. So I gave them a new salesperson that they were happy with and within 30 minutes they purchased one of our top products at the time.

One of the things I did do was make aware to the "smelly breathed" salesperson of his shortcoming. He was shocked and didn't realize it. So I asked him to verify with one of his colleagues concerning his breath and sure enough, he suddenly took it all in and knew he was at fault. But guess what, from that moment on, he spent extra time grooming and smelling good before he saw his prospects and never smelt bad again. He even thanked me years later and said I was the only one who had the guts to tell him straight about his breath problem, and he really appreciated what I did for him as it completely changed his life. Even his personal life improved. He made better relationships because he took the time to look after himself.

One small adjustment can alter the course of your success—forever!

A first and lasting impression is generated by how well you take care of yourself—how clean you are, how you smell, whether your teeth are clean and brushed after every meal. I have seen particles of food still lodged in some salespeople's teeth while they were presenting! This has cost them many sales. It's all the small stuff that champion closers make the big stuff!

Your Clothes

So how should you dress? Brian Tracy, a fantastically successful salesperson and leader said, "Buy half the clothes but twice the quality."

No, don't buy one trouser leg! He means buy quality clothing that lasts longer and looks good longer. Let me give you an important example. I spend on average $500 on one pair of shoes. My wife used to think I was nuts! She could not justify it. So, one day I listened to her and bought a $50 pair of shoes. They lasted two months and looked terrible no matter how long I polished them! My $500 shoes, however, on average last a good five years if properly maintained. My wife didn't complain anymore about expensive shoes. She knew then that they are a necessary part of looking good and professional.

What do bad shoes say about you? Well they say everything about you! The state of your shoes is what your prospects look at when they look at you. It's one of the last things they look at! So if your shoes have not been polished or are falling apart, what perception are you forming in your clients' head?

The state of your SHOES = The state of your CREDIBILITY and the state of your professionalism!

You think I am joking, or as John McEnroe would say, "You cannot be serious!" No, I am very serious! If you haven't got enough money to buy a decent pair of shoes, borrow the money because, in terms of clothing, it is the most valuable part of your attire!

What about the suit? When you wear a suit, a nice shirt, or blouse, follow the cultural grooming values of that country you are in. Personally, I love dressing in a suit and I make sure the suit I'm wearing is tailored to me—there's nothing worse than a nice suit that doesn't fit!

Now you can buy nice suits off the peg that are very reasonably priced, but please focus on the quality of the cloth you are buying. Don't buy cardboard-stiff material. If in doubt, buy Italian. They just always look the best.

As for ties, yes, I do wear them, but not all the time. However, for a first meeting with your prospect, I would insist that you do wear one. It's because at this particular point in time you do not know your prospect well enough to take liberties. Never assume just because your prospect sounds relaxed on the phone he has no problems with you turning up in jeans! That can be fatal.

A suit, a tie, and a nice pair of polished shoes tell your customer loudly that you care about yourself, you like yourself, and you always want to make the best impression possible. Proper dressing shows that you respect your prospects. They will like that very much because it shows you care about how they think and feel!

So Brian Tracy is absolutely spot on. Don't buy loads of shirts and ties; buy a few that will last and look fantastic! They will increase your income!

Now, I have not commented yet on the small things such as watches and jewelry and the reason I have not is because I don't consider them important enough. If you are ever seen wearing too much of this, psychologically what does it say? Gold necklaces, rings, bracelets, and diamonds can shout at somebody too much sometimes, so it is always best to "dress down" in this area. Focus on the suits and the shoes, and this includes the ladies.

Male and female should dress equally as professional. If the skirt is too short and the cleavage too visible, this can anger a prospect or distract them so much they will never focus on the service or product you're offering. Dress professionally and smart, this sends a message out that you are serious about what you do and you care about your prospects' feelings.

II. Creating a Solid Great Lasting Impression

How are you leaving your prospects after your initial meeting? What impression will they have of you so far? A lasting impression is being able to capitalize on the great first impression, and a great lasting impression is delivering what you have promised as a resource to your customer.

A great many salespeople always promise something during their presentation and at the end of their presentation, this promise can constitute a full proposal, agreement, or a tidbit of information and research the prospect has requested. It could be a very small thing such as your company's profile or some more detailed information about the product you are offering. However, you would be amazed just how many salespeople "forget" to follow through on them or just don't feel it's worth their time to go out of their way to get these things done.

On the contrary, they are very worthwhile because if you have promised to do something and you don't fulfill your promise, what kind of impression are you leaving with your potential prospect? You are leaving an "I don't care" message to them, that you are washing your hands of them, and in many senses you have already "burned your bridge" when you do this!

Now, a major footnote here: it is always better to close your deal on the first confirmed "appointment" where you have the opportunity to give your prospect a "full" presentation.

In Chapter 24, I will recap and brief you on these elements that you absolutely must be prepared to execute in your meeting but basically there are 17 steps to a successful "full" presentation. These 17 steps are done only after you have achieved rapport, something which the bulk of this book teaches. Although earning trust is paramount, keeping it is just as important and you will still have to keep building rapport throughout your presentation.

In the following chapters, I will spend some time preparing you in the content of the 17 steps, so by the recap you will be fully informed.

Be the DOCTOR of what you do.

When you are sick, too sick to tolerate any more pain, you will picture a doctor or a clinic in your mind and then focus your remaining energy to source the best doctor for your problem. However, many people go to the wrong doctor!

For example, if you have a skin problem, the general practitioner (GP) will prescribe a cream or an antibiotic for you. Yes, the problem will go away, but if it keeps coming back, your body is signaling that you need to find another solution or an "expert" for your particular condition, someone who can treat the cause of the sickness rather than the symptom. What people nowadays do to source this "expert" is ask their closest friends and family and/or search on the internet for a doctor who can help them.

Now the question is, how well do you know your field, or your area of expertise? Could you answer every question your prospect fires at you? Could you give them a good enough reason to trust that you know your stuff and that you were prepared to know your stuff to be qualified in attending to their needs and fulfilling them?

These are questions you need to answer, and you need to answer them with complete confidence. You also need to prove your "doctoring expertise" with sufficient research and evidence that is very convincing. In fact, convincing enough for your prospect to never ever question your credibility again!

When you first start selling, or you change to selling a different product or service, it pays to know your stuff and it pays to know and have a great relationship with other people in your company or industry who also know their stuff.

Friends, it's like this:

> **Your prospect will know within the first two questions**
> **they ask you if you can genuinely help them because**
> **you know more than them but, most critically, you**
> **know how to solve their problem or need precisely!**

When I say precisely, I do really mean precisely! The sad reason why many salespeople have been labeled "the lowest form of life" is because there are many "bulls****" out there—pardon my language—who are still bullsh**ting their wares all over the place! In fact, there are companies out there that specialize in "fooling" their target market, people who are of a certain level of intelligence who won't question the products' imperfections and limitations.

> **People's desire to get what they want can blind their**
> **judgment and cause them to end up with products which**
> **are totally unsuitable for them and don't fulfill their needs!**

Because most people have made this mistake in the past, they are frightened to repeat it! So they will ask many questions until, in their mind, you really are what you say you are and they know you can deliver. There is a famous saying which I would love to share with you. It's a little crude but it really drives the point home: "If you want the best steak in town, you're not gonna put your hand up a cow's rear and search for it. You're gonna take the restaurant's word for it!"

Well, isn't that interesting? The truth is, the prospects really want to take your word for it! They really do so much, however, be prepared for them to put their hand where they feel like it to search for the best person to fill their needs and solve their problems.

**They are going to search and they are only going to
stop searching when you have become their doctor!**

This is how you make a lasting impression! You can, of course, achieve a similar level of "doctoring expertise", especially when you are starting out in your industry, if you have a colleague or a resource within your group that you can leverage.

For example, if you are selling nutrition supplements and you don't have a degree in nutrition or some sort of certification, it is wise to know people who do. But you must ensure that they are accessible to you and that you can spend enough time with them to really learn why people trust them, or at least learn the pertinent and relevant information they know. Doing this will make you a CHAMPION RESOURCE to your prospect. Nevertheless, it is important to know this: it is not necessary for you to always leverage on other people's "doctoring expertise".

When I started a health and nutrition business last year, I had absolutely no clue about health and nutrition. I just spent 18 hours of my day, every day, with people who were experts. Within 30 days, whenever my contacts, friends, and family had health problems, they didn't go to the doctor, they just asked me their health-related questions and which doctors to go to if I didn't know "everything" about their problem! This has reached such a level that now referrals from my contacts call me first about their health and nutritional needs!

Why is this? Why do they do this? Did I bribe them?

Well, a loser's mind might think that way, but the truth is, I followed through. I gave my prospects and clients the correct information, and do you know what?

Their health got better!

Yes, I was amazed too! Not because I knew their health would get better. I had stuck my hand in that cow's rear many times before I got involved with these health and nutritional products that I now advocate. What I was surprised about was that they came to me first before going to their doctors!

The fact is that there are many great "doctors" out there, but there are also many "doctors" out there who don't know about certain nutritional needs, and they would rather prescribe a "proven" drug to alleviate the pain. This is especially sensitive when you understand that the average GP spends only one hour of their entire medical degree on nutrition! So, logically, if I had spent 18 hours a day for 30 days on studying nutrition, that would make me 540 times more knowledgeable on nutrition! Not rocket science, is it?

Now, I do add here something crucial to bear in mind:

If I don't know something, I will tell them I don't know, and then I would recommend them somebody who does know!

There is a limit to everyone's knowledge and "doctoring expertise". When you stay within your scope, you are perceived to be a master at what you do. As soon as you step beyond it, you become an amateur! So stay within your scope or learn a new field before you express your "doctoring expertise"!

Sadly, most salespeople can't be bothered to become that doctor. That's why they will never ever become champions. Champion closers know that acquiring "doctoring expertise" keeps them champions and consistently improves their income. It leaves a solid, phenomenal, and lasting impression on their prospects and clients without fail!

CHAPTER 20

CREATE DESIRE (I)

*"Sizzle the DBM! Create a sufficient
motivating want to buy your offering!"*

Whatever you desire the most, you will see a crystal clear picture of it in your mind, in its best light and in all its glory. You will see yourself benefiting from that desire with complete joy and ecstasy, with such intensity that you will keep seeing it until you have it. You won't stop this craving until you fulfill this intense need. You will have no peace and you will not sleep until it is your reality! This is your DBM, your **DOMINANT BUYING MOTIVE**.

The question is: How do you create that kind of "burning desire" for *your* product or service?

Do you want the simple answer? Of course you do! But first, you must realize without any doubt that everybody, in their mind, *thinks in pictures* and *not* words. Once you truly understand this simple fact you will know this:

Paint a clear picture in your prospects' minds of them benefiting from your product. Get them to see themselves benefiting from it. Keep painting that picture until they have the desire to own it without its price being the issue at all!

It is this one insight above all that distinguishes the champion closer from average salespeople who can't be bothered to spend the time to "paint this vivid picture". Average salespeople will say it's just too difficult, it's too embarrassing and too "flowery"!

Well, friends, if I were to tell you what the **real** "deal clincher" is out of all the tips I've given you so far, this would be **by far the number one** tip I could ever give you, because it makes such a huge difference in the sales process! It is also the most fun to do, because it gets your customers excited.

In this chapter, I will give you a few examples of exactly how you can succeed at this without feeling that embarrassment and frustration many losers constantly feel. When they feel embarrassment, they **stop** painting the picture and instead just rely on a computer graphics presentation to paint it for them! Such programs, no matter how snazzy and slick, will not paint that picture for you. If they actually could **create the necessary desire** for your product, we wouldn't be having this conversation now and you wouldn't be reading this book!

Although some presentation software with the correct content can add massive credibility to your presentation, your prospects still don't like to be asked a question from something without a heartbeat. Your prospects, as you know by now, need that human interaction and need to know that you care about them. So don't use the electronic presentation you have or a website to do all the selling and closing for you. It simply won't work; these tools alone will not create that desire for you.

Think in pictures!

I have already mentioned above that everybody **thinks** in pictures. It's not entirely true though. In reality, people think in **video**. That means moving pictures with all the sounds, colors, and movements.

This video creates the **INTANGIBLE EXPERIENCE** you so desperately need to communicate to your target audience. Because it's only when you are able to do this that you will create that special "feeling" which your prospects **must** have to make that decision to purchase your product or service... because they **feel** really good about it!

Tell the story, make the movie!

Human beings universally experience life as a movie. We can rewind that movie back to moments we want to experience again and again because they make us feel good. But the only way we can get that "feeling" back again is to relive it in some way. One of the ways a lot of us do this is to buy a movie we love and watch it when we are feeling down or want to experience a certain feeling again and again.

It is no secret that entertainers, especially big movie stars, get paid the most money in the world of any profession there is. The reason is that you are able to watch them again and again and **feel** what their movie characters are feeling. People pay big bucks to have those kinds of experiences and there is no sign of that ever changing.

So to really get your prospects' desire juices flowing, you must paint the picture and tell the story at the same time. Let me illustrate what I mean. A good while ago I was "looking" for a new sports car. I "kind of" knew what I wanted but I didn't know specifically. I mean, I knew it had to be black, it had to an Alfa Romeo, and it had to be totally unique and different. It had to look, as we say where I come from "the dog's bollocks", which translates in English to "Wow!"

After visiting many Alfa Romeo showrooms—and getting tons of brochures—I still couldn't find what I wanted. I was feeling really frustrated until one day...

The law of attraction to what you want when picturing it in your mind is an incredible force. I had been searching and one day by pure chance, if you believe that, I was driving to my office and I saw the most beautiful sight I had ever seen—I saw the car I wanted! I nearly missed it because that was a place I wouldn't normally stop at and I was traveling fast.

It caught my eye and impacted me so much I couldn't stop looking at it. Immediately, like a knee-jerk reaction, I slammed my foot on the brakes because I knew if I missed it, I would forever regret it. This caused a bit of a mess behind me, but luckily I just managed to sneak into a parking space and ran over to the showroom window as fast as I could without being squashed by any oncoming vehicles!

As soon as I got to the window, my jaw dropped at this incredible beauty of a car in front of me. I had to keep staring at it just in case it disappeared because it was indeed a sight to behold. It was turning around on a platform so I could see it from every angle and, wow, did it look mean and sexy.

It was deep black in color and sat quite low to the ground. It had twin headlights so well positioned that it looked like it was going to pounce on me at any moment. The body kit was fantastic and the skirting around the whole car made it look very fast but at the same time very classy and totally unique. It even looked great from the back because of its sleek shape finishing with subtle spoiler on top of the hatchback and the fabulous Alfa Romeo badge shining from the spotlights above.

The one thing I knew about this car was that I *had* to have it, and I would do **anything** to get it.

I was so attracted to that car, I went into the garage, walked up to the salesman, and said to him to give me the best price for cash… although I didn't even have the cash! I had so much desire I "knew" I would find the cash. So I left a 500 pounds "holding" deposit and said I would be back in two weeks to pay the balance. I was so confident that I said to the salesperson that if I couldn't find the money within two weeks, they could keep my deposit!

During that two weeks I literally saw as many prospects as I could and saved up the 12,000 pounds cash. I went to the garage two weeks later and bought the car. The salesman at the time was very shocked that I was able to keep my promise, as I was only 22 years old at the time. **But I knew what I wanted.**

What I didn't tell you is, during those two weeks, every day I would stop on my way to the office in the morning and sit in that car. And when I left the office every evening, even though it was late, I would stop by the garage and I would stare at the car for at least half an hour before I went home. I had to remind myself how much desire I had for that car and how I would feel driving it with my hands on the wheel and how all my friends would admire me.

That desire that was created within me manifested into a reality and made me discover that you absolutely must create a strong desire in your prospects for whatever you are selling.

Let's go back to the beginning of my story, where I said I stopped my car and saw the most beautiful sight. You see, from the moment I was telling you a story, one which told of my adventure finding the car of my dreams, it wasn't a long story by any means, but while I was telling that story, I guarantee that you started picturing me in your mind as I walked over to the showroom and what I did next.

That is exactly what I mean. You must make that movie in your prospects' heads. You have to tell them a story of one of your existing customers with a similar problem to theirs and how they solved it with your product. Then you have to paint a picture of them using your product to fulfill their need and your product being able to without a doubt succeed in that.

The picture which you paint is something INTANGIBLE to them, meaning it is something they cannot physically see, and if they can't do that then they won't be able to grasp it! So you have to make that intangible thing TANGIBLE to them so they can see it and GRASP IT!

Transforming the Unseen into the Visible

Let's take another example. Let's imagine you were selling a new type of pasta dish to your clients. It could be that you were selling to the people who work in restaurants that sell pasta dishes, or you were selling the restaurant owners a new recipe to sell in their restaurants, or you were selling to your customers who were about to order from your menu!

Let's imagine this pasta dish was called "Zagleoni". Zagleoni, of course, is something they have never tasted before, and to get them to taste it you will have to create a desire for them to put it in their mouths! It is intangible; they won't be able to grasp your Zagleoni concept until they "see" it and visualize it and "taste" it! Yes, you will have to get them to taste it before they have even tasted it!

How do you get them to taste it? Well, good news—it is easier than you think! The closest thing I can relate it to is like when your friends are telling you that they went to this fabulous restaurant the previous night and the food was superb, but in particular they had this new pasta dish called "Zagleoni".

Let's put it into a conversation and try two ways: **Version #1:** "Zagleoni is a brand new dish that is simply something you have never tasted before. The first moment you smell it you could swear it was spaghetti bolognaise, but then this new smell kind of hits you in a different way. It actually smells fruity, vegetable and bolognaisy at the same time all in one. The instant you get the smell, your mouth starts watering immediately in a complete reaction to this fantastic dish. In fact, you can't help your mouth watering, the aroma is simply wonderful.

"Once the aroma of this beautiful food has infected you, you can't wait to taste that first mouthful. So without delay you swirl the most unusual spaghetti fusilli-thin-shaped pasta onto your fork and the fruit, vegetables, and beef cling on to the pasta so you can taste the whole experience in one forkful.…

"When it gets into your mouth, the fruity taste is really noticeable. It's like tasting a hot blueberry sauce, then closely followed behind, the rich tanginess of a tomato-based bolognaise sauce, then the freshness of asparagus all rolled into one. It is simply magnificent! It is like having a starter, desert, and main course all rolled into one, but it doesn't give you that heavy feeling. If anything, it feels light and refreshing and most of all, very tasty, so tasty, you want it in your mouth for hours and hours!"

Now, did you taste the pasta dish above? Here's another way you could sell Zagleoni. **Version #2:** "Zagleoni is a fusion dish containing blueberries, asparagus, and beef".

Which would you choose? Which one would sell you? Which one would get your taste-buds going?

The answer is quite clear, isn't it? If you had a salesperson using number two, you wouldn't be using that salesperson for very long! Because "spiel" number two is just a fact, and facts, my friends, do not sell—benefits do!

When I was writing the description in number one, even my mouth started watering! I actually had to picture myself eating that food so I could describe it clearly in words, and that's the thing—you have to turn your *words into movies*! This is not difficult and certainly not impossible. The reason many salespeople don't do this is because they are not prepared to do it. They are lazy and they will never be champions.

If you went to a restaurant and the waiter described the Zagleoni to you in the way like in number one the Zagleoni would be sold out pretty quickly. Why? Because number one is appealing to your senses. Your five senses filter to your brain the experiences you have on a daily basis. They are "screaming out" for experience because your brain is constantly "screaming out" to learn new experiences!

People buy products depending on how they *feel* about them. They have to feel a product to grasp it. They can only grasp it when they "see" it and have desire for it.

The fact is that I just made the Zagleoni up. I have never tasted it as I made it up in my own head. It doesn't exist. But I do know how to show you the "sizzle" and get my customers excited, and I can only do this if I appeal to their senses and stick to the rules of creating desire.

Third Party Stories

Earlier in the chapter I mentioned that it is an excellent idea to also show and tell a story of one of your existing customers using and benefiting from your product. This is great because people generally don't like to be the first to use your product. They want to know that other people are successfully using your product already, and they want to know who they are. They usually want a list of existing customers but really they absolutely want to know that the system works for them, and the most effective way of doing this is to share with them an existing client's experience through a third-party story.

A third party story is exactly the same as painting the picture of your prospect benefiting from the product. However, this time, the story is of a third party using your product or somebody else that is not them!

Third Party Pasta?

Let's go back to Zagleoni's! This time, instead of just describing the pasta dish, you add names and places to the same story:

"My friends, Jack and Sarah, went to this fabulous restaurant while they were staying in New York where they were served this new dish called "Zagleoni". They were really surprised because the manager, a guy named Sergio, made a special visit to their table to describe it. And Sergio was so full of passion! Jack and Sarah sat opened-mouthed while he went on to describe it in this beautiful Italian accent: 'Zagleoni is a brand-new dish –ah that is simply something you have never tasted before. The first moment o you smell it you could swear it was -ah spaghetti bolognaise ah, but then this new smell a kind a hits you in a different way. It actually smells fruity, vegetable and bolognaisy at the same time -ah, all in one! And the instant you get the smell, your mouth starts ah watering immediate. In fact a, you can't help your mouth from watering, the aroma is simply wonderful—ah, *bellisimo*! (He kisses his mouth with his hand!)

"'Once the aroma of this beautiful food has hits you ah, you can't wait a to taste that first mouthful! You start a swirling this *bellisimo* spaghetti fusilli pasta on to your fork a and the fruity, vegetables and beef a get on to the pasta so you can tast-ah the whole experience in one-ah mouthful, it is simply wonderful!'

"My friends were so enthralled by Sergio's amazing explanation, Jack couldn't help asking Sergio what it tasted like: 'When it gets into your mouth-ah, the fruity taste is really as amazing you know, it is like tasting ah hot ta blueberry sauce, then is followed behind... erh, how you say, it is the rich tanginess of a tomato bolognaisy sauce, then the freshness of asparagus all rolled into one -ah. It is simple *magnifico*! It is like having a *starta*, desert and main course -ah all rolled into one -ah, but not heavy feeling, no no nah, if anything it feels, erhh, light and refreshing and, most of all-ah, very tasty, so tasty, you want it in your mouth for hours and hours eh!'"

Heh, heh, heh, sorry, I had just had a giggle then when I reread this passage. Isn't it amazing that the same passage as before can sound so different and elicit such a different response when we just change a few words and expressions? The inserted names, places, and Italian accent just make it richer and more believable. I have highlighted the accent in italics so you can refer to it to learn how it's done!

Did you now picture Sergio right then expressing his Zagleoni dish to Jack and Sarah? You just couldn't help it, could you? In fact, whenever I do this, every time the reaction from my friends has been, "Wow, I've got to go there! That sounds amazing!" When you are able to tell third-party stories like this to your prospects, they will eat it up and will have more desire for your product!

This above story is only for demonstration purposes. Use true stories of your prospects benefiting from your products and services. Build up a list of stories you can use at the most appropriate time. It will build your credibility and create more desire for what you are offering.

Using these stories is really called "sizzling the DBM". The dominant buying motive has to be discovered first before you paint all these pictures. If you are painting pictures of benefits that they are not interested in you will fail quickly. But as you know by now, you can discover their DBM by asking the right questions!

So let's lay out the five-step plan for creating desire. It's a plan you must follow to **qualify and earn the right** to close your prospects at the perfect times during your presentation.

CHAPTER 21

CREATING DESIRE (II)

"Five must steps to generating maximum desire!"

Below I am outlining the five steps necessary for generating maximum desire. I will elaborate and explain why each one is necessary as we go along. I've used these steps on every presentation for over 20 years. They have always been effective in creating the desire I needed to jump-start my sales and get the money rolling in!

1. Find the DBM (Dominant Buying Motive, or reason they will buy today)
2. Demonstrate your company and product can deliver
3. Show financial proof
4. Paint the moving picture
5. Close on peak desire

Remember these steps and keep repeating them until you master them as an integral part of what you do daily. We have already discussed some of them in earlier chapters, but let's do a quick, but detailed, recap here.

Step 1: Find the DBM

You must discover **what** your prospects' "most singular overriding interest" is in **using** your product and, most importantly, **why** that is important to them. The response to that question will be their DBM. The DBM is the reason for them to buy from you today.

The "why that is important to them" is crucial. You will have to use Level 1 and Level 2 questions to hone in on their critical buying motive. A fantastic question to ask is: "If I gave you a million dollars and said you could only spend it on your life insurance, what life insurance would you choose and why?"

Or a more **PSYCHOPEN** question (depending on the level of rapport) is: "If I gave you a million dollars and said you could only spend it on your life insurance, what three things **must** your life insurance have to make it perfect for you and your family." (**Note:** If you are not selling life insurance, you would of course tailor the question to fit the product.)

Please refer to Chapter 18 for these questions again and again and again, and when you have mastered it, please refer to it again! The response to these questions when you have super rapport can take you to the subsequent steps and truly assist you in "sizzling the DBM" and getting your prospects to really see themselves using your products and services.

Step 2: Demonstrate Your Company and Product Can Deliver

Reassure your prospects that your company can deliver their needs and dreams. Show them that what they want to do is readily available to them and that it is easy to use, easy to understand, and other people are using it successfully.

If they want to save time with your product, you need to fully demonstrate **how** your product can do that. For example, if you are selling a mobile phone package and your prospect's DBM is that she needs to get email quickly anywhere in the world and surf the internet quickly and use **Skype**, then you **must show them physically how they can do this!**

Too many phone dealers don't demonstrate. They are afraid to use the phone, they don't want to get it dirty, and more often than not they don't know how the phone works!

Let me paint the picture for this demonstration so you really get what I mean: You're in a phone shop and you kind of know what you want. Then nice and easy, the salesperson at the counter starts the conversation, smiles, asks questions, and listens carefully to your needs. You feel comfortable with this person since you know he has really spent the time clarifying your needs, then, because he has read this book and studied and has achieved the status of "Champion Closer", he asks you the DBM super question: "Ma'am, if I gave you 5,000 dollars and said you could spend it on the phone of your choice, what three benefits must the phone offer you to make it the perfect phone for you in the coming years?"

Possible prospect answer: "Well… it must be simple to use, I must be able to use it anywhere, without setting up, it must have a big screen so I can see clearly what I'm doing, and very important to me, it must have a long battery life because I travel a lot."

The Champion Closer can now focus on a demonstration of the perfect product, instead of showing ten phones! At this time, a **working** demonstration model must be available for use, demonstrating particularly those three buying motives the prospect has communicated, namely: simplicity, big screen, and long battery life.

At this point in time, it would be best to let the prospect surf the internet on the phone to her favorite sites. So you ask her what sites she visits most. It would be best to allow her to check her email on the phone you have so that she **believes** it is possible. And it would be best to allow the prospect to phone her friend from that phone to check on the voice quality using normal lines and **Skype**!

How many phone dealers do you know who will go that far to close the deal? Yes, I think you would agree, not many! And don't forget a phone is a tangible, physical item which can be touched and felt. The intangible elements include how it looks in the prospect's mind, and the working features of the phone when it is in operation! This is the key of reassurance. The prospect has to see herself using it successfully, then the phone starts to become an extension of her so she is less likely to leave the shop without buying it! In addition, you are also showing that you are an expert and authority when you are doing this. The prospect will trust you more.

At this point in your presentation, it's very common for prospects to start asking the price and the cost effectiveness of the deal. This is because as the "feeling part" starts to like it, the "logical conscious part" of the buying cycle has to justify the purchase.

Give them confidence.

Step 3: Show Financial Proof

Prove your claim with evidence, i.e. the cold, hard facts, because some logic is required to sell. You must use **FINANCIAL LOGIC** after you have completed Step 2—but not before. This will show your prospects that logically this product will save them money and that it does make sense.

So, at this point, they have the phone in their hand and they want to know the price. This is the time when you must have written or printed evidence that the phone and phone plan can logically save them money and be usable around the world. This will help justify their purchase.

This stage is critical in removing the prospects' fear of making a mistake for making the purchase. They don't want to go home with their lovely phone, start using it, and get a phone bill at the end of the month for the cost of their mortgage! This is more often than not what they are afraid of the most.

Now the Champion Closer at this stage would need to ask more questions on how the prospect intends to use the phone, but more pertinently, when, where, and for how long they are going to use it. The questions might go like these:

"If you don't mind me asking, Ma'am, to give you a clear indication of costs of this phone plan, I need to ask you a couple of questions on your usage pattern… is that okay?"

(Take your time, get permission, move on, keep rapport.)

"What times of the day do you usually make the bulk of your calls? Would it be morning, afternoon, night-time, or through the night?"

(We're asking trial close questions here which we will discuss in the next chapter. We are "closing the doors" to get to the "purchasing door".)

"Which countries do you travel to the most and how often do you make calls from those countries and where to from those countries?"

(The Champion Closer at this stage better have a calculator and the answers to these questions at his fingertips!)

When your prospects can see on paper an approximate monthly cost for using the phone they want for their exact usage pattern, they will feel **much better** and **much readier** to buy the phone and phone plan you are offering. You see most phone shop salespeople just give you the call rates, off peak and at peak times. Very, very few of them take the time to add all that up and show you the monthly cost! And how frequently do you get a phone bill? Do you get it every time you make a call? No, you don't! You get the phone bill every month! So the phone shop salesperson should be comparing monthly bills, not call costs!

Naturally, the forward-thinking phone shops would have a simple software system where the Champion Closer could input his prospects' usage patterns and show them on paper how it makes sense financially to do the deal! Remember how visual people are? Well, we all get bills, and if the phone shop salesperson **can prove** that the prospects' monthly bill will be cheaper through their package or more cost effective based on their usage patterns, that proof will convince his prospects that financially it makes sense. Then the potential money objection is taken away completely!

However, to really get the edge and clinch the deal, you must always push that little more and get that desire flowing in your prospects. You can only do this—and I'm saying this as an absolute, meaning, there's no other better way—by painting that moving picture!

Step 4: Paint the Moving Picture

Get your prospects to mentally see themselves benefiting from your products or services. **Sizzle the DBM!** We covered this in the previous chapter, but how do we create that moving picture with phone customers?

This is really simple because you can use the information you just learned from the prospect with the questions you asked earlier about her DBM, that is, why she wants the phone, where she will bring it, how she will use it, and when she will use it: "Ma'am, let's imagine you travel to Thailand, your most common destination for your business. You get off that plane, you feel very tired, you're shuffling through the passengers, and because it has been such a long trip, would you want the reassurance of knowing that your business is taken care of while you are away?" (The prospect of course agrees.)

"Well, one of the great features of this phone is that you can turn it on in Thailand or in any other country you visit and within seconds you can retrieve your email and messages using the cheapest network that suits your plan as it will automatically hunt the best one for you.

"You don't have to fiddle with the programming of the phone; it's all automatic. Your emails will arrive and you can download them at light-speed and see what you've been missing. Now you don't have to worry about phone costs and download time because your phone is programmed to locate a wireless system. In fact, your phone can download a list of locations for you on the move throughout the whole country, isn't that fantastic?

"The other great thing about this phone is that you don't have to get your laptop out of your heavy carrying case. Just find a coffee-shop, type in a password, and pay for that privilege. Wherever you are, you can download that excel spreadsheet you've been waiting for from the UK, and see the file directly on your phone, because the screen is so easy to read and navigate! How would you feel if you were able to do that when you get to Thailand?

"So while you're waiting for your luggage in the terminal, you can pass the time by reading all your latest business news and using the **Skype** interface for calling on the internet. You can call your daughter from Thailand completely free and let your family know you are safe and well, without worrying about the cost… is that what you had in mind?" (The "Is that what you had in mind" question is a Trial close to confirm their needs and hotspots because it requires a yes or no answer or a decision to be made.)

Suddenly the prospect asks a question (because she still wants her fears nullified), "What if there's no network and I can't get a signal, and it's an emergency?"

"That's a great question, Ma'am. What would you like to happen?" (Get the prospect to tell what she wants.)

The prospect may answer: "Well, I would like to know for sure that I don't have to worry about that, that there's some sort of feature I can fall back on in case of emergencies…"

"Totally agree with you and you're going to love this! You're in strange territory, you have absolutely no signal, you're starting to feel helpless, when suddenly you remember your phone has a special emergency SAT phone capability, meaning, you can use the nearest satellite to bounce a signal anywhere in the world.

"Fortunately you don't have to switch this on. Your phone will automatically detect you are in a danger zone and prompt you by a message or beep that you can use the SAT phone to call out and reach anyone in case of emergency. Now, if you're in Thailand, of course you're going to be worried that you can't get an emergency service, as you don't know the language, would you agree? (Prospect, "Yes, of course." You must use these **SMALL CLOSING QUESTIONS** to test the prospect is still with you. They are paramount in creating desire and closing on **peak desire**.)

"So, and this is a really cool feature, the SAT phone will be already programmed to reach an emergency number that will assist you when you are abroad, an English speaking 24-hour service, you can reach anytime, anywhere you are, and they will help in any situation. In fact, this feature is so cool that they can pinpoint exactly where you are with the GPS system built into the phone, and if necessary send someone to come and get you or direct you to a safe place by sending you the map!

"How would that make you feel if you ever got into that situation?"

Still at it, she may ask, "That would be fantastic it would really would give me peace of mind, but tell me one more thing, what if my battery runs out?"

"That is a great question, because normally batteries do run out don't they? (Wait for her response.) And you would feel quite insecure in a strange place, wouldn't you? (Wait for the response again.) How long would you like an emergency battery to last for?" (Wait for the response. Prospects would normally say in this conversation, "I need the battery to last as long as it takes the emergency services to get me!")

"We have seriously thought about that, and this is also very cool... in the event your normal battery gives out, you can type in a three-digit code to the phone to access the emergency batteries! That will last up to 12 hours on standby, your GPS location system will last for 24 hours... the emergency assistance guarantee without doubt that they can get to you anywhere you are within 6 hours! Are these features something you could use and benefit from?"

The prospect will probably say, "Wow, that is very reassuring. That's definitely something I need, but are these at any extra cost?"

"No, Ma'am, they are all built into your package!"

"Oh that's great!" she would respond.

"So, would you like the black version or the silver?" (Here, you are asking a Closing question and assuming they are buying just by asking what color preference they decide. Their response will tell you how much desire they have to buy).

At this point, the prospect's most probable answer is: "Oh, I think I'll take the black please."

Be the expert, paint the picture, answer every concern, eliminate fear, and close on their peak desire!

Step 5: Close on Peak Desire

By this stage, you will sense a strong desire by the body language of your prospects and whether they are asking questions about what you have just shared with them. When we painted the moving picture for the prospects, we targeted the hotspots they had in mind. And all the way through, we asked them small closing questions and trial close questions to see if the picture suited their needs.

For example, in the conversation above when the prospect suddenly asked the question: "What if there's no network and I can't get a signal, and it's an emergency?" We didn't carry on and ignore the question. Instead, we worked on her agenda. You see, this lady was already picturing herself in Thailand and one of her biggest fears was if she ever got stranded in the middle of nowhere, what would she do?

So instead of going on and on about more features, we asked her what she would like her phone to be able to do! We asked her, "That's a great question, Ma'am. What would you like to happen?" We get the prospect to tell herself what she wants!

The probable response: "Well, I would like to know for sure that I don't have to worry about that, that there's some sort of feature I can fall back on in case of emergencies…"

When you provide the opportunity for prospects to tell you what they want, they are telling themselves the benefit of owning your product! When they tell themselves the benefits, they "program" their mind to need your product and to desire it because it answers their questions and fulfils them!

When your prospects have talked about what they want, you proceed to show them how they can get it and paint the picture of them benefiting from it. Then, and only then, you ask a trial close! I will explain the significance of trial closes in the next chapter, but basically, a closing question goes something like any of these:

- "Is that what you had in mind, Ma'am?"
- "Would you like to see this feature in your phone plan?"
- "Can you now see why so many people are buying this phone plan then?"
- "If I could bundle all these benefits for less than what you're paying now, shall we go ahead?"
- "This phone is perfect for you, isn't it?" (A tie-down question.)
- "It's very easy to use, isn't it?" (Another tie-down question.)
- "Which one would you prefer, the black one or the silver?"

Always ask these **TRIAL CLOSES** or simple closing questions only when you have completed steps 1, 2, 3, and 4. As I have mentioned many times earlier, you can only ask people to buy your products or close them when they have "seen" the benefits, seen themselves actually **benefiting** from your product in a **moving picture** you have created in their mind, and when you have confirmed with them by asking trial closing questions.

> **Getting them to see themselves in that moving picture benefiting from your product is what sales is all about! You have to be an artist and paint colorful strokes and justify with a little bit of science or logic. Then, and only then, can you close them on peak desire and… Know when to close the deal and suddenly grow rich!**

When you have mastered these skills, you will be a Champion Closer and you will grow rich quickly. Your income will shoot up because you took the time to realize that it is only through creating desire that you will achieve big numbers and, ultimately, benefit your prospect so much more.

You may be thinking all this takes too long. Yes, I agree with you, that everyone's perception when reading this chapter is that it would take so long to sell that phone to that lady in the way I have illustrated. But, here's a little fact for you: **I was the one who sold that phone to that lady… in 7 minutes!**

Is that really too long?

SECTION V

MONEY IN THE BANK

CHAPTER 22

CLOSING SKILLS

"Confirm the deal!"

W e have already learned that to close effectively we must ask closing questions at the right time and in the right way! But what questions should you be asking? How do you know the right questions to ask when you need them? And more importantly, what is the psychology behind the questions?

In this section, you will see those questions in action. You will also understand why they are so crucial in creating that buying decision and that vital "Yes" from your customer at the end of the presentation.

As Champion Closers, we know there is a process we must follow. There is a closing process, but this only follows the **OPENING PROCESS**.

In previous chapters, I have stressed a lot and demonstrated why you can only close people when they are totally open with you and open about your product. You now have those tools and you will be so very happy when you start using Level 1 and Level 2 questions and see how easy it is to generate rapport and earn the right to advance to creating desire.

As the age-old adage goes, "the cart does not come before the horse", so must rapport be achieved before anyone will take the time to allow you to paint that moving picture for them. By using these strategies, you will see an increase in your prospects' desire to buy from you. You will be shocked by the kind of response you are suddenly getting! When that happens, it will feel really, really good!

However, this excitement will be short lived if you are unable to capitalize on this sudden desire you have found in your prospects! Remember, they are not customers until they commit money to purchasing what you are offering. Until then, your bank account will be groaning with inactivity no matter how excited you are and they are.

This is the time to be a Champion and stop losing. This is the time to ask them to buy. This is the time to bank the commission and start changing your life forever! This is the time when you need to close, because they already have the desire. Now they need to know what action to take and only you can lead them there!

And you can only lead them there through closing questions!

Imagine yourself as a great painter who has just finished a work of art. The paint is still wet. Now you must fix each stroke until you can move on to the next stroke. If you don't do it, this fantastic desire you have created will be washed away, and you'll have to start all over again! This is not a joke. Many a time I have seen excited salespeople lose the trail because they failed to close and solidify the deal at the right time. Or they failed to get the signature and follow through correctly.

Closing is a science. You must know when to ask the right type of closing question once you have earned that right, i.e. once you have built rapport and got their desire fired up.

And I say again, there has been much written recently about too much emphasis being placed on closing, that it is not necessary, that it's manipulative.

And, yes, I agree with this, except with one proviso: closing is necessary at the right time.

However, if you talk in percentage terms, I would say it is only worth about 15 per cent of your entire presentation. The majority of the time and effort, the 85 percent, must be spent on rapport and creating desire.

CLOSING SKILLS

RAPPORT BUILDING
& DESIRE BUILDING

Yet that 15 percent is the tip of the spear.

It holds all your great work together, and without it, that spear will be blunt and useless! Blunt and manipulative closing is common and ineffective. The closing techniques you are about to learn will make the difference between an income of five figures or seven figures—and yes, I mean in USD!

Let me begin by showing you the most common closing question you'll be asking, the "trial close".

CHAPTER 23

TRIAL CLOSES

"A perfect excuse for your prospect to make any decision"

A trial close, simply put, is an opportunity for prospects to make a small decision. Yes, you read that right: "a small decision".

Every salesperson thinks that the biggest decision prospects can make is the buying decision at the end of the presentation—and this would be the case if you have not asked them to make any decisions before they get to the buying decision at the end!

But, if you give them opportunities to make enough small decisions throughout your presentation, then they will find the decision at the end a small and minor one and one that makes logical sense as they have made already made the decision to buy IF you've done your job like a Champion!

If you do not ask your prospects any decision-making questions, such as trial closes, the decision you ask them for at the end of the presentation, i.e. the decision to buy, will be an extremely difficult one for them to make. It would be like trying to get blood out of a stone! Why do I say this? It's because if your prospects cannot see the benefits of your offer no matter how good it is, there is just no way they will buy at the end. They cannot psychologically and emotionally justify a purchase if they are not ready to buy!

Effective Trial Closes

A trial close is a closing question such as: "Would you prefer the extra international special assist insurance package?"

Now, if we use the mobile phone example from the previous chapter, when do you think this question would best serve the prospect's buying process? Before you paint the moving picture of the special assist insurance, or after you paint it?

If you ask this trial close question before you have created desire for the special assist package, they will not answer yes. They will answer either, "No, thanks", "I'll think about it", or "I'm not sure as I don't really know what it is"!

When you ask this question after you have created the picture of them lost in the jungle and special assist rescuing them and saving their life, they will most definitely say yes, because now they can see themselves in that picture you have created. So, the trial close question here would be: "Can you see yourself benefiting from this special assist program?"

If you have done your job, they will most certainly say yes here. Now, if you ask this further trial close: "If it were cheaper than your existing phone plan would you like it in your new plan?" and they say no, then you haven't done your job fully, because this question removes the price objection immediately!

So a TRIAL CLOSE is a closing question that tests your prospects' level of desire for your offering or one that tests your level of rapport!

Tests our level of rapport? Yes, tests our level of rapport. You see, you cannot ask people direct questions unless you have rapport with them. Otherwise, they will feel that you are interrogating them, and they will tell you it's none of your business!

Recently, I referred a car finance specialist to a friend of mine, Glen, who wanted to buy a BMW pretty quickly. When the finance specialist telephoned Glen, he asked him a few direct questions without building rapport first and justifying why he was going to ask him questions!

The finance guy just proceeded to ask Glen questions like: "What's your budget?", "What deposit can you afford?", "You want a 2005 or 2006 model?", and "Can I take your details?"

Obviously taken aback by such a "crude" approach, my friend Glen told him that it was none of his business and hung up!

So a trial close really helps you to assess the level of desire in your presentation, and it's usually a question that requires your prospects to make a small decision about their interests and needs in your offering. If they don't answer the trial close question positively, that can only mean you have very little rapport and desire!

Let's look at the two diagrams below. Diagram A shows the result of not asking questions in your presentation. You may have painted the moving picture, but because you have not confirmed with your prospects their level of desire and rapport, when you ask them to buy at the end, they will be nowhere near ready. It's like you put a pan of soup on the cooker and forget to turn the gas on. When you go to taste it, it's too cold—it's not ready! So you have to start all over again and warm it up!

In diagram B, you can see by the small steps in the diagram that you have asked lots of trial close questions. Each question you ask allows your prospects to make a small decision. Each positive decision they make takes them another step closer to the buying decision. For example:

—Graph A—

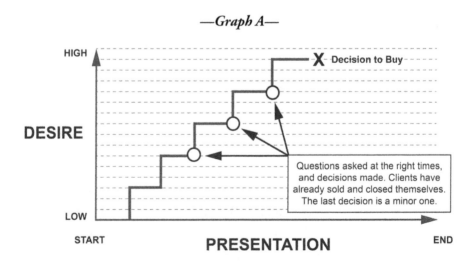

"Would you prefer a beach holiday or a city centre holiday?"
"So you prefer to pay by credit card then, MasterCard or Visa?"
"Would you prefer a one-bedroom apartment or a landed property?"
"Would you prefer a MP3 phone or an internet phone?"
"You would prefer the special assist package?"

—Graph B—

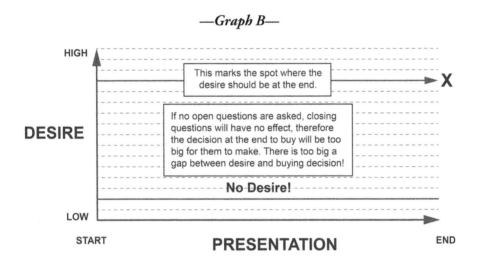

Alternate Choice Trial Closes

Sometimes, people call a trial close an "alternate choice question", because you are actually giving your prospects a choice between one preference or another, for example:

"Would you prefer the black or the silver one?"
"Would you like the off-peak plan or the business plan?"
"Would you prefer the Apple or the Sony?"

You have to imagine your presentation as a series of doors. These doors represent the choices the prospects have to make throughout your presentation. When they choose one door and go through it and their desire is there, you need to close that door behind them firmly shut, so they cannot change their mind at the end! If they start unraveling their decisions and options at the end of your presentation, it means you really haven't closed on desire; you have closed them using manipulation!

Remember to close the door firmly shut only when you have achieved the optimum level of desire from your prospect!

Tie-Downs

Oh my goodness! You have to tie them down? Not literally! A TIE-DOWN is closing the door firmly shut and locking it with a tie-down key. It's the commitment your prospects have made on their own decision and preference. Let me give you a simple illustration.

You:	Would you prefer the Apple or the Sony?
Prospect:	The Apple.
You:	Yes, I can see now from what you've told me, the Apple is really more suited to your needs, *isn't it*?
Prospect:	Yes, I really like using it.
You:	Know what you mean, fantastic to use, *aren't they*?
Prospect:	Yes, they're fantastic!

Can you spot the tie-down words and questions here? Let me point them out to you. The reason I have to point them out to you like this is because it's just a natural part of the conversation. It is not a manipulation. It's so easy to do this, but so effective in closing your prospect!

Look at the second question you ask them: "Yes, I can see now from what you've told me, the Apple is really more suited to your needs isn't it?"

I have italicized the tie-down at the end of this question: "isn't it?" These two words are so powerful in gaining a stronger commitment on the decision you are getting, because they have to answer a positive. It's a strong, natural closing question, one that makes their decision firmer.

The next tie-down in the above example is at the end of the next question you ask them: "Know what you mean, fantastic to use, aren't they?"

The "aren't they?" is the tie-down. Tie-downs are powerful closing tools to be used at the right time in your presentation—the time where you have lots of desire.

However, they are not the only tool. One of the best strategies I have ever used and still use today is explained in the next chapter, and that is "SAY-SHOW-SHARE." It's an awesome strategy because it gets the prospect talking about the benefits and selling to themselves!

CHAPTER 24

SAY-SHOW-SHARE

"Allow your prospects to sell to themselves!"

Wouldn't it be unbelievably fantastic if your prospects could sell to themselves? You know, they kept talking about the benefits of your products, became raving fans, and just couldn't stop!

Well, if you think that will never happen, you are dead wrong! In this chapter, I will show that it is paramount that your prospects do talk about your products, because when they talk (and listen to themselves), their belief level increases dramatically as your product starts to become part of them!

So, what is TELL-SHOW-SAY and how does it work? The truth is that it's not a new strategy at all. It is new to many salespeople, however, since they don't use it because they think it's not necessary to get prospects to talk about the benefits!

SAY (Belief Level = 10 percent)

If you just tell your prospects the benefits and how wonderful the product is, how would they know? I mean, the only person they have heard it from so far is you! They haven't seen independent evidence of it yet. And because they have only just met you and you haven't created super rapport yet, their belief level is naturally low.

The biggest mistake of any salesperson is when he stops asking questions and just tells the benefits to his prospects. This is a lazy approach, but ironically, it actually takes more effort because now you are doing ALL the talking and it bores your client because they are not involved!

SHOW (Belief Level = 60 percent)

Showing is backing your statements up with facts and cold, hard evidence. When people see this evidence, they become more convinced of your argument. For example, if you told your friends there was an earthquake in your town this morning, they probably wouldn't believe you. But if you showed them the headline in the national newspaper the following morning, I think you will agree that their belief level would rise dramatically!

When you are able to show them evidence—testimonials of other people benefiting, your website, demonstrating how your product or service works—it really does impress the logical side of prospects' brains. It justifies what you are telling them so that they can believe it!

SHARE (Belief Level = 95 percent+++)

But, by far, the most effective stage of this process in your presentations is when you are able to get your prospects to repeat, discuss, and get excited about your products in their own words.

People believe more of what comes out of their own mouth than what comes out of your mouth.

In this regard, this strategy is so effective that it increases their belief level to nearly 100 percent. And when they start talking about it, they are going to start asking you questions. They are going to give you buying signals because they are customizing your product in their head to fit their needs. If it doesn't take a lot of customization, they will get more excited by your offer! So let's get back to our phone shop...

When we asked the prospect if she would like the assist abroad package, she gave a resounding yes! But now we need to get her to say why she wants it. By getting her to tell herself why, she will become more convinced and that will solidify her choice because now she can picture herself using it.

A great question to ask at this stage to get the prospect talking about the benefit is this: "Ma'am, if you don't mind me asking, why would you really like the assist abroad package?"

The customer's actual response was, "Well, I feel it would really suit me because if I get stuck—God forbid—I know I'll be safe, and that's very important to me!"

To get an even stronger response, you could ask, "Ma'am, if you did get stuck, from what I've told you already how would you use the assist abroad function on your phone? Just to see if you got how easy it is..."

She answered, "Errm, it would be great, because I could just press this little button here on my phone to access the satphone. It would give me great confidence because I know I could get through and speak to someone in English and I know for sure they could get someone to me within a couple of hours, so that would be fantastic!"

Yes, just in case you were wondering, this was what the prospect said when I asked her these questions!

Can you see how this lady is telling herself the benefits, how she is justifying and picturing herself using that phone? This is the ultimate way to sell all your prospects! This will get you the best results of any strategy you use, because all you are doing is asking open-ended questions on the benefits you have just shown them. It is conversational; it is not an interrogation. It is something you would normally say and your prospects will not know or be aware of what you are doing, because to them, you are being completely transparent!

So to get your prospects selling themselves, just ask them how they would use your product and most importantly, why they would use it. Remember, the "why" leads to their DBM more than any other question!

If they cannot answer your how and why questions in this context, ask again. If they still don't answer, that means they have not been listening, you have no rapport, and there was certainly no desire created.

If they don't ask you any questions or give you any objections, that usually means they are not interested. Objections are fantastic by the way. That's why we are going to look into that in the following chapter, where you will learn how to overcome easily all the objections you will receive during your presentations!

Remember, this is the most important thing: what your prospects say, they will believe. At every opportunity, you must encourage them to speak about the benefits themselves. They will then sell to themselves and you will find that it is so much easier to get a commitment from them.

CHAPTER 25

OVERCOME ANY OBJECTION

"Welcome any objection as it shows interest from your prospect!"

Like it or not, in your presentation with any prospect, you will get at least one objection. Some prospects will give you a lot more objections than others. Over the years, I have discovered, although they come in many forms, there are only three main types of objections:

- "I'm not interested."
- "I want to think about it."
- "I can't afford it."

Salespeople who are not Champion Closers interpret an objection as a negative sign from their prospects that they just don't want to buy their product. So every time they hear one, they kind of give up. The reason I know this is because I used to do this a lot before I became a Champion Closer!

This misinterpretation is probably the biggest mistake salespeople can make when they are with their prospects. Because it is simply not true!

Objections actually indicate a genuine interest for what you are offering. Why am I so sure of this? Because from my experience, successful, qualified appointments have twice as many objections as unsuccessful ones! This is interesting, isn't it? The fact is that an objection is just another form of question your prospect is asking you. Remember what you learned in the previous few chapters? That any sort of question from your prospect is utterly fantastic, because that means they are totally engaged with you in your presentation!

When your prospects start objecting, it means that they are beginning to consider your offer very seriously. This is when you have created an opportunity to sell!

Yes, an opportunity, because you have created a chance for you to listen to them and build more rapport. Plus, you now have an indication of where they are in their buying process and what they do and do not like! The paradox is, most times, you absolutely cannot sell without objections!

You may wonder now, "What if I'm not getting any objections?"

Well, if your prospects are not objecting or disagreeing, then most probably they will not buy. Why? Because they are not taking you or your product or service seriously! If they were interested, they would show inquisitiveness and compare what you are offering with something they already have or know about. To compare, they must have a frame of reference. To have a frame of reference, they must know the fundamentals of what you are talking about. They must be more aware of what your product or service is, otherwise they won't risk spending their hard earned money, to be more aware they must ask questions to clarify in their own mind and realize exactly what your offering is and could mean to them. This is human nature and part of anyone's buying cycle.

NO OBJECTIONS = NO INTEREST
LOTS OF OBJECTIONS = GREAT INTEREST

Most direct salespeople misread a lot of objections as a lack of interest when quite the opposite is true.

> **A warrior does not fight an opponent who is sitting down and not interested in battle. He sits down and waits... [Ju-jitsu warriors' philosophy]**

In other words, you can only convince somebody when he or she is engaged with you!

But where do these objections come from? They come from prospects who are basically not convinced yet of your offering, whether it's on the phone or face to face. They just don't want to make a mistake in buying or subscribing to your offering.

> **Therefore, what's driving the prospects to say these comments is fear.**

The fear is that your service or product will not solve their problem and they have to waste their time and money through the whole process of your presentation. It's just easier if they told you they were not interested!

You may not think that's fair to you, but let's have some empathy here. How would you feel if you purchased the wrong product? This question is important because we are all programed to hate making mistakes, especially if other people depend on your product purchase.

> **An objection is a concern. A concern comes f rom interest. And interest comes from desire!**

How do you know when they are interested and engaged with you? That's easy! They'll be talking, objecting, and asking questions more than you are! Objections are what people use to understand your offering and justify logically if it makes sense. If it makes sense logically, then it will feel more like the right decision for them. Then, emotionally, the prospects will feel secure in their purchase.

**People make decisions based on how they feel,
and not how logical it is or may seem.**

If it's not logical, the emotions do everything they can to justify the decision. Eventually, their emotions cannot reason with their logic, and the prospects won't be happy because they are having an internal struggle.

You must satisfy emotion and logic needs before your prospects buy.

Experts believe 80 percent of their first decision will be emotional. It will have to feel good when they buy. Logic takes control when they are not under the sales influence, when they get home and reconsider. To avoid them telling you they need to "think about it first", you must satisfy this question during your presentation: does my product make sense in the cold light of day to them?

To overcome any objection, you must always use these four laws:

- Always agree with their objection.
- Always understand where it is coming from.
- Always listen fully to their objection, even if it is very negative.
- Always clarify it before you respond and try to overcome it.

Law #1:
Always Agree!

Yes, and this is one of the most difficult things you can ever do, because it's really tough agreeing with people when they are not happy with one of your products, your industry, or even your competitors who sell similar products!

For example, a prospect tells you his friend bought one of your products and had a bad experience with it, and if you disagree with him, you would be calling him a liar! Any time you allow yourself to do that, the sale will be lost, because you will have destroyed rapport.

Such feedback from a prospect doesn't mean he's not interested. It just means that he wants to protect himself and prevent himself from making a similar mistake. This objection allows you to listen to him and fully understand where he is coming from and why he said it.

I say again, always agree with them, but you don't have to directly agree with them, like saying, "I agree with you!" You can say this instead: "You know what? If my friend said that to me, I would absolutely have the same concern as you right now. I completely understand why you are saying this."

Can you see the big difference? In the first response, if you had said directly that you agreed with them, they would think there's something definitely wrong with your product because you agree with that concern. In the second response you have understood their concern!

Law #2:
Always Understand Them

Seek first to understand where this objection is coming from. You can only do this by agreeing with it first, listening to them, and asking them a question to clarify it, e.g., "What product did your friend buy and what problems did he have exactly, if you don't mind me asking, I would love to know."

A lot of the time they won't remember, and in some cases, it will be a product from your competitor that they have mixed up in their own mind. This is usually a great opportunity for you to differentiate yourself from that competition. What an excellent break your prospect has created for you! So do work on understanding the objection completely by asking them enough questions.

Law#3:
Always Listen to Them Attentively

…even if what they are saying is negative! After agreeing with them, now you really have to listen to them fully, and not stop listening until they have finished! This is especially true if a prospect is in an angry mood or is raising his voice to make himself heard. People who are shouting do so because they want someone to listen to them. So you must do just that AND LISTEN if you want to be a Champion Closer.

This is one of the most challenging exercises for most salespeople since they just want to butt in because they too start to get angry when someone is shouting at them.

This is the worst thing you can do at this stage, because it will inflame the situation into something much worse!

When you listen to them fully, they will start running out of steam. And when you keep agreeing with them, they will start to trust you and begin to tell you the real reason behind their objection.

They will become emotional, but then will start to calm down. This is absolutely essential in responding to complaints and objections in any sale you are attempting to close. You definitely cannot close until you have overcome these objections. They are part of the process! Let your prospect run out of steam and say everything they need to say before you respond to them!

Law #4:
Always Clarify an Objection Fully

…before responding to it. That means you have to really understand your prospects' words and then repeat to them that you understand what they mean. They need you to fully understand them and you can only do this by asking more questions about their objection.

For example, if they tell you they feel they can't use your product, you need to clarify why: "What is it about the product you feel you cannot use, the assist abroad feature, or another part of the phone?"

Actual response: "It's really the cost I'm a bit worried about. If I have all these benefits I can't afford it."

Now in this instance you have a response and you have another objection which is completely different from the first. So we would call the prospect's first objection here "smoke". This SMOKESCREEN has been hiding her real objection—that she's afraid she can't afford it!

For your information, people put up smokescreens and change their objections very often! It is only when you are willing to clarify with them that you will allow them to give you the true objection—in this case, money!

Your response to this new objection should be something like this: "So, correct me if I'm wrong, Ma'am. You like the phone, the plan is good and safe for you, but it's the price you are worried about? Is that correct?"

Actual response: "Yes, that's pretty much it. I love the phone, but don't know if I can keep up the monthly costs."

"Ok, now I understand. If there was a way to reduce your monthly payments to a comfortably affordable level, where you didn't worry at all about the payments and kept most of your plan that you want, would you go for the deal?" (This is an excellent trial close question that addresses her concerns and objection.)

Actual response: "Yes, that would be great, how do you do that?"

At this point, you have overcome the objection and gotten her interest back! Can you now see why objections are the "sexiest" response you can ever get from your prospects?

**It is the consistent and determined effort that breaks
down all resistance and sweeps away all obstacles!**

Here's another common objection: "I'm not interested." So what do we do? Well, use the BRUSH ASIDE method!

"That's all right. Most people in your situation felt exactly the same way when I first called them. But all those people have become our best customers, have thanked me for introducing them to this fantastic product, and now they recommend us to all their friends! Why? Simple, it is helping them achieve their goals much more easily!"

This will normally trigger the response from the customer, "What is it?" to which you respond, "That's exactly what I would like to talk you about and I only need 30 minutes of your time."

**Listen to every objection without interrupting,
because listening builds trust!**

Treat every objection as if it were a question. When prospects say, "I can't afford anything" say, "That's a great question! How can you justify the price at this time? Let me see if I can answer that for you." Then proceed to earn their attention by showing them what benefits they would get if they won the product in a competition... For example, what you could say is, "I totally understand your situation and thank you for your feedback and time, but tell me IF you had won this product in a competition FREE how would you use it?"

This gives your prospect the opportunity to tell themselves the benefits of your product, then allows you to create more desire for the product. The "I can't afford it" objection is very commonly a smoke screen for something else, normally the fact that you haven't created enough desire for the product yet, meaning they can't see it benefitting them yet!

However, average sales people give up at this objection all the time because they are too lazy or don't know how to create enough desire at the right point to know when to close the deal!

The All-Time Greatest Responses

There are three great responses to any objection that have withstood the test of time:

1. "How do you mean?" This question is nearly impossible not to answer! You can also say, "How do you mean, exactly?"
2. "Obviously you have a good reason for saying that, do you mind if I ask what it is?" Often the prospect does not have a good reason for objecting and this will help clarify it.
3. The Feel-Felt-Found method.

For instance, if a prospect says, "It costs too much," or "I don't have the time," you can say, "I understand exactly how you feel. Others felt the same way when they first heard the price or offer. But this is what they found when they began doing the business and using the products and service..."

Then go on to explain how other customers found that the benefit or value of your product more than justified the price you were charging. This means that this stage would be a great opportunity to show them real live testimonials of other customers you have sold to and how they found your product/service.

It would also be better and more powerful if you showed them real testimonials of people in their own industry or with the same problem as them and they will relate far more effectively.

So you see, objections are the best way to test the temperature of your prospect so you can tailor the nest part of the presentation you are going to give them, down to the questions you ask and content you show them and knowing WHEN to do what you need to do!

Demonstrate that the benefits they receive greatly outweigh what they are paying. Tell them how other customers FELT when they heard the offer and started using the products.

If you asked this question: "I could sell to every prospect I spoke to if he or she just didn't say…"

Practice the answers to this question and build your repertoire of answers to handle objections and they will never hold you back again!

You will learn very quickly what objections to expect and learn how to overcome each one. The simple fact is that the more objections you overcome, the more chances you will get to present the true benefits of your product/service and the more sales you will make!!!

Champion Closers absolutely *love* objections!!!

CHAPTER 26

CREATE URGENCY

"It is always better the prospect buys now, why wait?"

Y ou have completed your presentation, you have created desire, you have asked all the right questions, you have listened with care to your prospects, they want to buy, but they are not buying! They are giving you reasons to put off their purchase, even though they have said to you it's what they really need. They have even told you they can afford it! So how do you motivate them to buy now rather than wait and keep waiting?

In all my years of selling, I have learned that there has to be a legitimate reason for your prospects to buy now. What I mean is that it has to make sense to them to buy now rather than wait!

It's interesting to note that if you've got money in your pocket which you have worked extremely hard for, you won't want to let it go easily. It's natural to hold on to the money. Most people love having cash on them. It makes them feel secure and happy. So, for your prospects to give you that cash for your product now, they must understand that it will most certainly improve their lives now and solve their problems now!

What I am saying is that the value (or perceived value) of your offer has to be greater than the value of the cash in their pockets or bank account.

That means they believe and know they will get far more return in dollar value by buying your product than keeping the money in their pocket! To give you their cash, they must first SEE they will get that value back!

So how do you create urgency to buy your product today without manipulating or creating false reasons to? That's a great question because many unscrupulous salespeople will invent "offers" to entice their prospects which are not really true. For example, have you ever heard of this offer? "If you don't decide within the next seven days, the price will increase by 20 percent!" Then you find out a week later that it hasn't increased 20 percent. It was just a lie told by the salesperson to get you to sign on the dotted line.

The Law of Scarcity

The law of scarcity states that if you know something is not easily available, is running out, or might never be available at that price again, you will desire it more, because it creates "a sense of loss" in you. That sense of loss motivates you to act now! Psychologically and emotionally, you actually see yourself far more clearly not benefiting from the product you want to buy because you have already seen yourself benefiting from it earlier and it felt so good.

A great Champion Closer knows he can only motivate the prospect to buy when he has created the moving picture and that peak desire, otherwise he cannot create urgency to buy now.

Have you ever tried taking a lollipop away from a small child and seen the emotional reaction, that sense of loss for him? Kids are incredibly powerful at displaying this sense of loss!

You desire something more that you know or perceive you can't have!

Let me give you a great example of this. In Kuala Lumpur, Malaysia, the city where I live, the government increased the fuel price by over 40 percent in one day! Yes, you heard it correctly, 40 percent. That is a huge jump. But they did not announce it in the newspapers. They sent the message out very quietly that fuel would "likely" increase by midnight the same day!

On that day, I never had the chance to see the news because I was busy in a seminar. However, I knew something was "different" that evening because it took me five hours to get home where it would normally take me only 30 minutes! The reason it took five hours was because I was stuck behind miles of cars queuing at every gas station in town to pump their tank full of petrol at the price they knew or perceived they would never see again!

My point is this: if your prospects know your offer solves their problem and they really need it, and you are giving them the best deal you can and they know that they won't get the same deal in the future, in their mind it will make sense for them to buy now and not later!

However, let me get this straight: if you are giving a limited time offer, make sure it is a genuine offer. And please justify the offer with a good enough reason or they will smell a rat and run away as fast as they can!

If people are going to get their cash out, they also need to know they are getting a special deal. Most people I know, including myself, will not get their cash out unless they are getting a special discount or offer on that day to buy. The prospects have to see financially that they are winning on the price of your deal just as much as you are winning.

Every deal you make has to be win-win in an equal relationship, never win-lose in your favor.

The great thing is that it doesn't have to be a huge discount. It just has to be something the prospects feel they have won from you, and that no one else has gotten the same deal. This is where the law of scarcity works so well and so effectively each and every time you apply it to your sales process.

Nonetheless, the real sense of urgency is generated when you are able to really focus on your prospects' needs and really listen to their problems. In this sense, you are not a salesperson but a counselor—a consultant working for them.

You are on their side and you are advocating a solution to them!

Why do people go to advocates and solicitors? They go for impartial genuine advice. In this respect, as a Champion Closer, they must trust you to advocate to them the best product for their needs and the best solution.

It's like this: my best friend is an emergency physician in an Australian hospital and his job is very intense. He has to make split-second decisions every day and he is under tremendous pressure to offer the best solution to his patients. If one of his patients came into the emergency ward and said to him, "Well, thanks for the recommendation, but I think I'll think about it first," that patient would most probably die for making such a decision to procrastinate!

Think about your prospects' true needs. Is your product going to improve their lives and solve their problems? If you know it is and you know for sure that if they don't buy, you will be doing them a disservice, you have to create urgency in the sense of making it very clear why they should buy now by repeating what they have already said to you during your presentation, word for word. For example, "Ma'am, you said to me earlier it is very important to you to know you are safe at all times, and in case of emergencies you need to have a system you can rely on, can you see this system working for you today?"

Restate and repeat exactly the same words to them which they have said to you, then ask them a trial close question to confirm that it is really what they need. They will answer you positively.

Secondly, and one of the most powerful questions you can ask, is ask them what their life would be like without your product. Now you are creating a sense of loss: "Ma'am, if you were stuck in a very strange place with no phone signal and your battery was running out fast and you had no food or water, what would you do without this system?"

This is an extremely powerful, emotional Level 2 question. The response to this question will determine if they really have the desire and need for your product. So you paint the picture of life without your product! And this creates a sense of urgency to your prospects!

Special Offers

There is absolutely nothing wrong with special offers and limited time packages—if your product suits your prospects' needs perfectly and will genuinely benefit them. In such a case, there is no reason why you cannot offer an extra incentive to buy now. And contrary to popular opinion, it doesn't have to be a cash discount.

If it is a website subscription and you give two extra months for free when they sign up now, that's a great incentive that doesn't cost you any money.

If you sell cars and you offer a free service and free valet (car cleaning and shampooing), it won't cost a lot of money.

If you sell mobile phones, giving away a free carrying case or some extra credit will not hurt your profit margin.

All these are great offers, but the key is that they must be genuine and for a limited time only, which will not be repeated. Once your prospects know this, the sense of urgency will kick in.

Do these really work? Yes, they absolutely do work, and sometimes if you don't offer a discount or a deal, you won't get a sale that day. Like it or not, people do need that extra reason to buy now. It has helped me a lot and still helps my sales team now! Meaning, people don't change their buying process!

Everybody wants discounts and special deals, and if you don't give them, your competitor will and take your market share!

Here's a quick urgency guide to help you remember how to create that urgency to buy today!

Quick Urgency Guide

1. **Create excitement in your voice!**

    Enthusiasm accounts for 51 percent of your sale. The last four letters of enthusiasm are I-A-S-M, which stand for "I Am Sold Myself"! Show them you are sold on your product and company. This creates a sense of urgency to join you, because if you believe, they will want to believe.

2. **Share with them that lots of prospects are buying your product and share with them why.**

    Prospects also have to know others are buying your product and that they are totally happy with it and it has changed their lives for the better. Show and share some of these existing clients. This creates a sense of ease to join you as others have already jumped over. This generates a sense of urgency to jump over to you too, because they don't want to be left out!

3. **Find their DBM and other hotspots.**

    I have said it before and I will say it again: find that dominant buying motive, that real need your prospects need to satisfy. Ask questions to find and listen to their answers in full!

4. **Repeat their needs to them.**

    State back their needs to them word for word. This shows you have been listening and that what they need you can supply easily and readily and they can have it now! This creates a sense of urgency to get rid of that pain and fill that need they have been aching to fill.

5. **Take it away from them.**

    Create a picture of life without your product! Yes, when you have created desire in your offering, you now have to "take it away" from them. Get them to really picture what it would be like if they didn't have your product. If they show regret and a sense of loss, this will create more urgency to buy now!

6. **Create value-added limited time offers.**

    Always offer something extra as a reward for buying now. Let them win in the negotiation process. This can be offered on the day only in very direct sales or for a limited time in retail or on-line environments.

7. **Have courage in your conviction!**

Add conviction to all your communication and have no fear when asking people to buy your products. The confidence you express will communicate to your prospect that it is normal to buy on the day or in the limited time period, and that other people have easily made that decision before. This will make them more comfortable and will give them more trust in you to do business now instead of waiting.

CHAPTER 27

MEET AND SUDDENLY GROW RICH

"Find prospects who need what you are offering at light speed!"

U p until now, we have discussed what you need to know to succeed at closing deals. However, if you have no one to present to, you will have another sad trip to the ATM looking for money that isn't there in your account!

Having learned how to be the best and do what is necessary to be a Champion Closer, you must also know how to find those hot prospects who really need what you are selling and are willing to pay the price for your product or service.

I know many great closers who know how to present and close but they just don't have enough prospects and qualified customers. Their appointment diary is not full; they have too many gaps between appointments, and these people still wonder why they are not making the big bucks.

Let's get this very straight:

Sales is a numbers game!

Very simply put, this means the more qualified people you see, the more business you will generate, and the more revenue or cash you will attract!

If your closing percentage is 50 percent, which by the way in general terms is an outstandingly good figure, but you are only seeing two prospects a week, then you will only close one deal a week on average. If, however, you are seeing ten prospects a week, that sales figure suddenly shoots up to five sales a week! This is a huge difference in terms of how much commission you will take home every month.

To show you an example of this difference, let's imagine you are selling vacuum cleaners at $500 apiece and the commission is 50 percent. That is $250 a week, even if you close at 50 percent because you are only seeing an average of two qualified prospects weekly.

If, however, you are closing five deals a week, selling five vacuum cleaners, that is a jump in commission to $1,250 a week. Now we both know what you would rather have—everybody would rather have the $1,250... except the losers of the bunch. They would see making more appointments as too hard and too long a job as they think they won't have time to see all those prospects, let alone present to them. But the strange fact is this: the people who have made more appointments and have seen more people will actually have to spend less time making appointments!

How is this so?

Well, what we haven't really talked about yet is the simple method of generating REFERRAL CUSTOMERS from existing clients!

When you are seeing more people, and more people are buying from you, those same customers will be happy to recommend their contacts because you have taken the time to locate them, present to them, and ultimately sell them a fantastic product which really helps them. You would have essentially created a bunch of RAVING FANS, who are so necessary in building a fantastic sales career and a great business. And the more times you present, plus the knowledge you gain about your company, your product, and ultimately your customers' specific needs, means you start to demonstrate that you are an AUTHORITY in your industry and you will be perceived as an expert! We know authority removes the fear in prospects from buying from you.

Once you have reached this level, you don't have to spend two days on the phone speaking to cold prospects. (By cold I mean you have not met them yet, they don't know you, and you don't know if they are even interested or qualified!).

When you have QUALIFIED REFERRAL PROSPECTS, you have struck gold in filling that funnel full of cash-generating spending power that keeps refilling on automatic mode because you have developed a great referral system based on your B.R.A.N.D.! Your B.R.A.N.D. will now literally attract others to follow you instead of you chasing them!

Your B.R.A.N.D. generates your referral engine!

Let's first have a look at the funnel you have to fill to start your engine!

So now you know, without a qualified prospect there is absolutely no chance of a sale, no chance of building rapport, and definitely no chance of presenting and closing people who do not exist! That is why one of the most common questions I get asked is: Where do I find more qualified prospects?

Before that fantastic referral system kicks in, you have to know where to meet those prospects! To do this successfully, you must first understand these three laws:

1. Prospects do not come to you without knowing about you.
2. Prospects do not come to you without a clear benefit for them.
3. Prospects do not come to you without you asking them to!

How will the qualified prospects know about you? Well, where do you normally meet people in your everyday life? If you are in a certain job, you will usually see people in the same industry daily, e.g. colleagues, suppliers, bosses, and existing customers.

But how do you meet new people?

To generate a new lead or prospect, you must penetrate new networks and groups that you are not in right now and you have to network better with the existing people you already know.

This is the time where you must reveal your true NICHE and determine your value and relevance to your targeted prospects!

Let's start with the people you know and your own circle of influence. As I said before, to succeed and become a Champion Closer is not rocket science. It is a simple process that, once followed, can be repeated and duplicated to grow your sales and grow your business.

It is generally estimated that each of us by the age of 18 have met and known casually around 2,000 people! Yes, you read the figure correctly! However, the way you met those people and their impression of you will determine how strong your relationship is with them and how far you can LEVERAGE those relationships. The simple truth is that every relationship is leverageable and I don't mean to sound cold here like you are taking advantage of people.

A relationship you can leverage well is one which you have given significantly to before without thinking about what is in it for you. That means very simply that you have invested in that relationship, you have developed it, and you have nurtured it.

Let me illustrate this clearly. Please read the following few paragraphs carefully on how to build relationships successfully:

True friends give you love, trust, and the most glorious opportunities you could ever imagine without ever thinking about getting anything in return. They always have you in mind whenever they meet anybody else and are your walking, talking, free advertisement—an advertisement that is the most powerful message you could ever wish for, the kind you could never afford no matter how much money you had because this advertisement is totally genuine: there are no hidden messages, no gimmicks, no promotional special offers. It comes straight from the heart of someone who thinks very well of you. This advertisement comes from a person who believes he knows you and that you are a person he can trust, or that you have inspired him in a very significant way and he simply wants to tell other people how you did that, how you helped him make a change in his life, a breakthrough he had been searching for, etc.

To this day, I am still totally and utterly surprised how many people underestimate just how valuable a close and trusted friend can be. They pay no heed to how big their own circle of influence is by way of their own communication channels and how many people they can touch in that process.

Far too many of us practice a level of indifference in our everyday activities that would shock our grandparents! It stems from a warped belief and attitude that we don't need to talk to anybody we meet as though we cared. We don't have to talk to the cleaner, the bus driver, the student, the housewife, or the child and the teacher, or any other human being whom our society surmises and labels as having occupations that are of little significance and contribution. Indeed, how on earth could these people possibly benefit me and further my goals? They are not important enough to warrant special attention from me, so why even bother?

This kind of thinking and behavior has also, understandably, given a lot of people antipathy of so-called worthwhile and meaningful occupations, such as politicians, lawyers, and businesspeople, and especially the individuals doing these jobs. This kind of perception has resulted in the much commonly used thinking pattern of "well, they don't give us any respect so why should we?" It has led to a certain skepticism and a level of distrust which is very challenging to break indeed, so much so that very little effort, if any, is ever expended on changing these perceptions. It is tragically an accepted part of our everyday lives.

It is also very sad that even the people in the world of high flyers, the movers and the shakers, find it very difficult to trust one another in case the other person tries to pull a fast one on them. This is such a strong perception that more often than not people do try and pull a fast one and create even more distrust and bitterness!

It really does not have to be this way at all. Aren't we taught in business and for the quality of our own lives to co-operate more, to have more WIN-WIN relationships? I believe we would all be astonished to discover just how many of us are not practicing this!

And this is the thing about any successful relationship that will last a lifetime and stand any test it may be subjected to:

> **You should never think what is in it for you to get to know another person. This should never be the first thing on your mind! What should be on your mind is how much you can SERVE the other person. The more you are willing to SERVE without ever thinking of the reward you will get back, the more you will receive in return!**

Yes, it is a paradox. When you take away the expectation of getting something back and the people you are in the relationships with can see that for themselves—that is, they totally believe you are genuine, that there is no hidden agenda—then that is the defining moment, the moment when you will have real trust and the most beautiful and rewarding relationships you ever thought possible! This is true both in business and in your personal life. I can say this with such conviction because I have experienced it many times. My generosity, kindness, and genuine interest in the other person has paid me back time and time again. It has never failed me. I am a very rich man in this respect, a very rich man indeed. I am filled with the most wonderful relationships life could give me and I am eternally grateful for this.

> **People are looking to see if your actions truly reflect your beliefs and totally match what you are saying. They need to connect to the real you, the person whom they can trust.**

The person you are talking to is really thinking: Why I should trust you? I can't form any rapport or do any business with someone I don't know or trust.

There are many different kinds of fear when two people first meet, but the dominating concern is usually this: I don't want this person taking advantage of me, that's why I'm holding back. I don't want to tell them everything yet. I need some kind of signal for me to let go.

There are many different stages of any friendship or relationship. These stages reflect many different behavior patterns. But remember, it is never the other person's fault that he (or she) is not as close a friend as they potentially could be.

The only way another person can start to trust you is by believing that you genuinely care about him and that you are not just thinking about yourself. Again, this is true for both personal and business relationships. This giving creates a reciprocal relationship where your friends will love to give you referrals because you have gone out of your way to help them and given them referrals.

And when your NICHE is clear, your friends and contacts will see your value is well worth the effort of recommending their friends to your product or service. Why? Because they know it will benefit them and of course the direct benefit to the person referring you is that they know they are serving their friends, and when you serve, you feel the greatest of all—you feel like a billion dollars!*

I may have ranted a little here but I needed to make this point clear: great contacts and relationships like you emotionally and mentally and would love to reciprocate your assistance and kindness by giving you their help and connecting you to their network. These are the people you should be talking to first, and to really talk to them, you have to start sharing what you do with them!

Now you may be asking yourself what is the benefit to them for listening to you rant on and share about the things you do. Well, the fact that they are listening to you means they feel more valuable and worthy. Their self-esteem will increase because you asked them for a chat to share more. They know there is a great chance you could help them. You already know this because I have discussed it in this book many times and repeatedly so far!

To share with people what you do, you have to understand what you do clearly, so they can understand you clearly! Again, we have discussed that you must be clear in your communication for people to have clarity when you are talking to them. Because once you are clear, it is so much easier to share.

And, of course, the backbone of sharing and what makes people get excited over what you are sharing about is your enthusiasm about it. Enthusiasm generates more leads, more interest, more appointments, and, ultimately, more sales. Remember the last four letters of enthusiasm? I-A-S-M, or I Am Sold Myself! Once you have nailed that enthusiasm, your appointment making becomes a breeze! It becomes an easy and enjoyable part of what you do.

So let's put first things first in prospecting! Here are six steps to a full schedule!

1. Master your B.R.A.N.D.
2. Understand fully the benefits of what you are doing and what product or service you are selling.
3. Learn and master the process of building rapport and presenting.
   a. Complete a goals worksheet (i.e. how many sales you need to generate the income you need).
4. Create a list of names of people you know and can share with.
   a. Connect with them (i.e. call them, email them, see them), SOUNDBENEFIT them! (Note: read further to see what I mean by this.)
5. Share the benefits with all you know.
6. Follow through and generate referrals.

Qualifying

Always bear in mind to never think about closing them before you meet them. Always share first and then see who is interested in the principal benefits of what you do. This is how you qualify which appointments to set first!

Lots of salespeople believe qualifying is all about if the prospects have the money to buy what they are offering. Now part of this is true because there is no point presenting to somebody who is not the decision-maker or who does not have the money to buy.

However, before you can even do that, you must know who can benefit from your offering. The matter of decision-makers and budgets is after this.

What many salespeople forget is that even if the person you are sharing with cannot benefit, he may know someone who could, and if you have given without thinking of receiving, he will gladly give you those referrals! And if you are really smart, you will also give him referrals for his product or service. That will make you more valuable in that person's eyes, translating into: you are someone really worth talking and listening to!

Reciprocation develops a great referral market!

Once you abide by this strategy, your lead base will grow. That growth will seem very slow at first and, most times, it will seem as though you are going backwards and not forwards! But if you are willing to work really hard and smart, at some point within weeks of you starting this new way of doing your job and business, you will see yourself reaching a critical mass, an unstoppable momentum, and suddenly have a full appointment book!

Qualifying is using your time efficiently to generate the most suitable prospects for what you are offering.

Talking about the benefits first gets their attention and filters out those who are interested and those who are not!

So how do you BROADCAST your new niche, value, and relevance to your target market? Only two ways:

OFFLINE and ONLINE!

Traditional OFFLINE methods are:
- Calling them
- Texting them
- Meeting them face-to-face

Doing it ONLINE includes via:
- Your website (on exactly what you offer, your niche, etc.)

- Social media (Facebook, Instagram, Snapchat, Twitter, etc.)
- BUSINESS COMMUNITIES (Linked-In, etc.)
- Emails (from your own email contacts)
- Online video media (YouTube videos of testimonials and demonstrations of people benefiting from your product or service)

When you do this, you must in the first line of your communication tell them the benefit of what you are doing, meaning the potential benefit to them. This is called your SOUNDBENEFIT (which I mentioned above under "6 steps to a full diary"). For example, if you have just opened a mobile phone shop, you might start with this line: I am now supplying the hottest mobile phones at the cheapest prices guaranteed to save up to 35 percent on your calls!

You can do this both offline and online and even put it on your website and create a Facebook community by in-house communication to your Facebook friends, or by very cheap, targeted online advertising. (By the way, if you still don't have a Facebook/Instagram/Twitter/LinkedIn account, then you are a dinosaur that is about to become extinct forever!). Make sure you create ALL of those social media accounts, they are the four major channels, where you have the opportunity to BRAND yourself and be seen by your target market, and being seen is regular posting on the subject you are the authority on... Keep your personal life away from social media, be sociable and a great resource to the people that really need your products and services.

Facebook and ALL social media is free, and the people on Facebook love to communicate online. Your target market in demographic and psychographic (the reasons people buy your product and service) terms are most definitely present and actively looking for your service or product! Social Media is HUGE and is growing so fast—I am talking millions of people a day! You will miss the biggest opportunity of your life if you don't learn how to use it. (It's actually easy, but if you need more information on this awesome tool, subscribe to www.marcorobinson.com and learn by receiving free articles about this and many other relevant subjects.).

Or, if you are in real estate, you could say: "I have a waiting list of qualified cash buyers if your property fits this criteria..."

Or, the business I am in, which is wholesale incentive vacations: I now supply $1,000 holidays for only $10.

These are one-liner SOUNDBENEFIT sentences that are designed to get people's attention and raise their interest level. These kinds of lines generate qualified appointments because you are making your prospects very curious and expanding their need to know more about what you do because it could potentially benefit them greatly.

So, when you establish your website and online communities, you can engage people online about your services and products, create transparency, inspire trust (because you are using it as a mechanism to build rapport), ENGAGE their desires, and start to create demand!

People are always looking to make money, save money, and do things in a more convenient way.

Once you give them a line and you can follow through after you have stated that benefit, meaning you can also demonstrate credibility, you will succeed—guaranteed because you are satisfying a need. This is the qualifying and prospecting part of your funnel.

Appointments only follow once you have successfully networked, prospected, and qualified. It is a simple filtering process.

Now you should be able to easily create a list of 100 names of people you know well. Start calling them now, have a conversation, ask them how they are doing and how you can help them with their business, and let them ask what you do. When they ask you what you are doing now, you are not pushing an appointment down their throat, you are generating interest. And if you noticed, I said ask them how you can help them first. This encourages them to feel better and more confident dealing with you on a regular basis.

This is a great way to network when you meet people at events, business clubs, and parties because you either already know them or you are meeting them face to face, which enables you to create rapport more effectively. Always start with the people you know first, ask for their valued opinion as a friend what they think of your products and services, practice and present to them, and your referral list will build exponentially.

When you are approaching a cold market, it is more difficult to get appointments because you don't know them and have no rapport or relationship built yet. However, you can still generate interest from new prospects with those one-line SOUND BENEFITS in advertisements or door knocking and, of course, with your online communities and websites (that have keywords and phrases). So when people search in Google what they are looking for, your website and online presence will come up if you have written those one-liners and website copies well! And if you don't know how to do that, learn how to do it and leverage from the people who have mastered those skills. (Hint: Step #1, join www.marcorobinson.com!).

Door knocking is the most fantastic way to learn how to get people's interest at super-speed and gives you the ultimate no-nonsense feedback because if they are not interested, they will tell you by closing the door in your face! However, the more times that happens to you, the more times and opportunities you have to really learn from those mistakes you are making so when your referral list has really grown you don't need to knock on doors again!

To generate lots of appointments from people who want to buy from you, you have to:

1. Generate a qualified interested lead
2. Contact that lead within 24 to 48 hours and make the appointment
3. Ensure you arrive early to your appointment
4. Know your product well and clearly
5. Be ready to present confidently
6. Earn the right to ask for a referral at the end of your presentation.

And again, you need to have mastered your B.R.A.N.D. beforehand!

Once you follow these easy steps, it is a very simple process to keep that appointment diary full. One other thing I must add is this:

**Make your appointments for the following
week on Thursdays and Fridays.**

When you are able to book the following week's appointment slots on these days, it gives you a far better chance of having that diary full. This is because by the time Monday comes along most people have already filled their schedules for that week and you will find it very challenging to get your prospects' attention on the phone on a Monday morning as that is usually when they don't have the time to see you or arrange to meet you.

Do it on the last working days of the week as most people generally have more time and are more relaxed at this stage. Besides, it is great because then you are not panicking over the weekend because you don't have anyone to see on Monday!

Making appointments this way is not limited to offline or face-to-face meetings; you can also very easily do this online! You can digitally attract people to schedule time with you on chats, Skype, or online web-conferencing in audio or, better still, video! And of course to all the budding internet marketers out there, you can sell online, you can create web sales copy and videos online that sell and convince people they should buy from you, whether it is from your website or from your online communities which you have created and developed, seeded and populated, or engaged and fulfilled.

People do want to buy online. All you have to do is master your online B.R.A.N.D. and ensure that it complements your offline B.R.A.N.D. so effectively that when you deliver that communication correctly, you can literally—and pardon the overused cliché—make money while you sleep and create an automated, online, money-making system! There are many Champion Closers who have already achieved this milestone and have left their competitors far behind in their wake.

Remember in the beginning of this book, I said that your ability to learn was your number one, greatest asset? I still say that and will always say that! If you want to reach the heights of seven-figure monthly incomes you need to turbo-charge your learning speed and join the club of high-flying empowered individuals.

I suggest and strongly recommend that you start doing this by joining our community at www.marcorobinson.com and fully develop your B.R.A.N.D. online and offline—and funline! Yes, because it is no good making lots of money if you don't know what you are making that money for! Your reasons and purpose have to be compelling and be able to fulfill you in every single way!

So when you are well on the way, you must enjoy and have fun in the process of it all, otherwise what is the point in taking the journey?

See you on the bright side at our next Marco Robinson conference. Until then, to your sublime success!

ABOUT THE AUTHOR

Marco Robinson is a number one best selling author, award winning entrepreneur acclaimed author of the #1 bestsellers *Close The Deal And Suddenly Grow Rich!* and *The Financial Freedom Guarantee* & now has his own Prime Time TV Show "Get a house for free".

He is also the World Record holder of most sales in a month and year in his industry of membership sales, a world-renowned accomplished speaker, and appears regularly on national radio and TV.

From a direct sales background and with no formal or university education, Marco has achieved over 1 billion dollars' worth of business sales (as reported in the New Strait Times on Sep 9, 2009), taken a public company from $10 million to $500 million in three years in the previous economic crisis. He is also founder of Naked Dollars (NAKED Technologies: www.naked.technology) and has had ten years experience in building successful businesses, which have successfully sold $500 Million worth of investment products, these products have included properties, travel, education and more…

Marco Robinson, now even has his own Prime Time TV Show on Channel 4 in the UK "get a house for free" where he has been able to give houses away to the homeless and underprivileged and is using his new cryptocurrency and blockchain, naked technologies, to make homelessness obsolete!

Please check out Marco's prime HIT TV show excerpt here:
https://youtu.be/ukpim8INIxg
Please see his story live on the BBC Breakfast Show:
https://youtu.be/IYpndqG0t8Y
To read his entire, updated bio and get great tips and expert opinion, go to his website www.marcorobinson.com or just follow him on his Twitter, Instagram, Facebook or Linkedin links.

Join his new website community for FREE (www.marcorobinson.com) and join many others who are breaking new records in their own industries because they have read this book and also attended Marco's incredible workshops.

CHECK OUT THE BACK COVER OF THIS BOOK
TO RECEIVE A FREE ONE DAY WORKSHOP WITH
MARCO ROBINSON LIVE WORTH OVER $1,000!

Morgan James
Speakers Group

www.TheMorganJamesSpeakersGroup.com

We connect Morgan James published
authors with live and online events
and audiences who will benefit
from their expertise.

Printed in the USA
CPSIA information can be obtained
at www.ICGtesting.com
JSHW022216140824
68134JS00018B/1083

9 781683 509110